SpringerBriefs in Business



For further volumes:
http://www.springer.com/series/8860

Daniela Venanzi

# Financial Performance Measures and Value Creation: The State of the Art

Springer

Daniela Venanzi
Department of Business and Law
University of Rome III
Rome, Italy

ISSN 2191-5482 e-ISSN 2191-5490
ISBN 978-88-470-2450-2 e-ISBN 978-88-470-2451-9
DOI 10.1007/978-88-470-2451-9
Springer Milan Heidelberg Dordrecht London New York

Library of Congress Control Number: 2011940802



Printed on acid-free paper

Springer is part of Springer Science+Business Media (www.springer.com)

*To my parents, for their never fading support*

# Contents

# Introduction

The periodic measurement of firm's performance is conducted for several reasons. From an external standpoint, it helps investors in formulating their expectations concerning the future earning potential of firms. From an internal standpoint, we can list the objectives according to Vancil's (1979) framework: (a) it helps managers decide where they should allocate their resources (*operations evaluation*); (b) it supplies a plausible feedback on how well the company and its sub-units have achieved their goals (*activity evaluation*); (c) it furnishes the basis of an adequate bonus plan that gives incentives to achieve the firm's goals and rewards the results of proper decisions (*managerial evaluation*).

The measurement of corporate financial performance in terms of accounting-based metrics, has been viewed as inadequate, as firms began focusing on shareholder value as the primary long-term objective of the organization. These metrics fail to take into account the factors that drive shareholder value. Value-based measures were therefore created: they explicitly acknowledge that both equity and debt have costs, suggesting the incorporation of the financing risk-return into performance calculations.

The focus of this book is providing a systematic review of the most known value-based measures: the **economic value added** (EVA) described by Stewart (1991), the **cash flow return on investment** (CFROI) of the HOLT Value Associates/Boston Consulting Group and the **shareholder value added** (SVA) described by Alfred Rappaport (1986) and the LEK/Alcar Consulting Group. For the sake of completeness, the **economic margin** (EM), formulated by the Applied Finance Group (Obrycki and Resendes 2000), and the **cash value added** (CVA),[1] that is a registered trademark of FWC AB (Weissenrieder 1998) are also included in the discussion.[2] Both represent a sort of mix of some of the main metrics above.

[1] But it should not be confused with the CVA derived by the CFROI.

[2] All cited metrics are registered trademarks by the respective consulting firms and their rights are all reserved. Now CFROI is a trademark of Credit Suisse Group.

Conversely, metrics that are very similar to one of the main measures are omitted, like McKinsey's economic profit, for example, that works much like the EVA.

Information and empirical results about the efficacy of the different approaches are limited and contradictory and seem to be primarily provided by authors with strong commercial interest in the outcome of any research into the effectiveness of the methodologies. On the one hand, consulting firms have been battling for the last two decades over the superiority of their value metrics, stating that competitors' measures have flaws that compromise their evaluation ability. On the other hand, a growing number of firms have adopted various economic value measures, moving from one metric to the other over the years and often abandoning all of them in favor of traditional accounting measures.

In sum, despite the increasing emphasis on these value measures, no definitive evidence exists of which metric works better than others do, and research on the extent to which any of them is superior to traditional accounting measures is limited and not yet univocal.

In this scenario, the objective of this book is contributing to the on-going dialogue on the appropriateness of different value-based performance measures, by providing a systematic and updated framework of their respective strengths and weaknesses and by summarizing and systematically comparing the main international empirical evidence on their effectiveness. It would be a mistake to believe that any single measure is perfectly suited to all types of financial decision support, while it could be very useful to *compare* the different measures. We will point out both their differences and their similarities, adopting different perspectives, from which their respective effectiveness can be evaluated: (1) measurement logic; (2) association with market financial performance; (3) consistency with the discounted cash flow (DCF) approach in measuring value creation; and (4) implications on managerial incentives.

The book can be a powerful tool for guiding managers and graduate students in the "tangled forest" of the existing metrics, by providing them with the quick, but adequate, knowledge and skills for "piloting" the choice and the use of these measures, instead of being passively dominated by them.

The book is organized as follows. First, we summarize the shortcomings of the accounting-based measures of performance. Therefore, we illustrate the economic value measures, pointing out their differences in calculation. Subsequently, we compare the economic value measures' effectiveness from three different perspectives:

a. the empirical evidence on their association with stock market measures of return: the objective is comparing the relative extent to which the different value-based measures predict stock returns;

b. their linkage with the DCF approach, in order to verify their consistency with the economics of value creation;
c. their impact on management behavior when used in compensation systems: the key question here is whether the use of economic value measures, for internal decision-making, performance measurement, and compensation purposes, improves organizational performance.

A final summarizing scheme of the strengths and weaknesses of the value-based metrics will conclude the analysis.

# Chapter 1
# Criticism of the Accounting-Based Measures of Performance

**Abstract** The traditional accounting-based metrics are not consistent with value creation and do not handle any of the four factors (i.e. investments, cash flows, asset's economic life and cost of capital) on which value depends. Therefore, managing for short-term earnings compromises shareholder value. In this chapter, the fundamental shortcomings of the accounting-based metrics are discussed, focusing on the following aspects: subjectivity of the accounting figures, inconsistency with the goal of maximizing shareholder wealth, and short-termism of managerial decisions.

**Keywords** Shortcomings of accounting-based performance measures · Accounting return versus economic return on investment · Economic depreciation

## 1.1 Introduction

Value is a function of the following factors: (1) investments, (2) cash flows, (3) assets' economic life and (4) cost of capital. The mechanism that is used in the market to establish value using these four factors is what we call the **discounted cash flow** (DCF) approach. This is the reason why we use DCF methods when we evaluate the investments that a company plans to make. The objective of doing this is to be able to establish and execute strategies and investments that increase shareholder value. But in practice something peculiar seems to occur (Weissenrieder 1998) after the investment has been made. Companies, analysts and media abandon this thinking and enter the world of P/E-ratios, earnings per share, ROI, balance sheets, P&L statements, book equity, goodwill, depreciation method and so on. It means that we try to follow up the value creation and profitability of the investments that we have made by using accounting data. Rappaport (2005) calls this "disease" the *short-term earnings obsession*.

D. Venanzi, *Financial Performance Measures and Value Creation: The State of the Art*, SpringerBriefs in Business, DOI: 10.1007/978-88-470-2451-9_1,

Accounting does not handle any of the four factors the way a financial framework should handle them. What kind of information does the organization need for strategic decision making and for managing the company's current operations? Choosing the accounting approach for the only reason that it is what we are used to would be a mistake. Managing for short-term earnings compromises shareholder value. In the following sections the fundamental shortcomings of the traditional accounting-based metrics, both as value creation measures and performance measures, are summarized.

## 1.2 Inaccuracy and Subjectivity of the Accounting Numbers

The accounting principles provide companies with room for manipulating the accounting figures. Earnings figures may be computed using alternative and equally acceptable accounting methods: a change in accounting method for financial reporting purposes can materially impact earnings but does not alter the company's cash flows and therefore should not affect its economic value. This could have two implications:

- comparisons among different firms as well as different years of the same company are not reliable.
- managers can assume *moral hazard* behaviors that can induce various manipulations of accounting data. The Graham et al.'s 2005 survey (more details below) of 400 U.S. financial executives reveals that companies manage earnings with more than just accounting gimmicks: a surprising 80% of respondents said they would decrease value-creating spending on research and development, advertising, maintenance, and hiring in order to meet earnings benchmarks. More than half the executives would delay a new project even if it entailed sacrificing value. Managers push revenues into the current period and defer expenses to future periods: they borrow from the future to satisfy today earnings targets. Jensen (2004) cited WorldCom, Enron Corporation, Nortel Networks, and eToys as companies that pushed earnings management beyond acceptable limits to meet expectations and ended up destroying part or all of their value. Cirio and Parmalat are similar examples in Italy.

Moreover, accounting figures can be distorted by inflation: in determining traditional accounting measures of return, we put together heterogeneous figures, i.e. numbers not expressed in the same monetary unit. For example, inflation can increase ROI by increasing capital turnover (while sales are expressed in current values, invested capital is not). On the contrary, measures based on DCF calculations are not affected by inflation: in determining value-based measures of performance it is enough to use homogeneous figures (real or nominal) of cash flows and discount rates. Therefore, ROI could depend on the average age of the fixed assets of the firm.

Despite the International Financial Reporting Standards' (IFRS) attempts to reduce the possibility of such manipulations, valuation methodologies such as "mark-to-market" tend to exacerbate the problem.

## 1.3 Nonalignment with the Goal of Maximizing Shareholder Wealth

Accounting-based measures of return omit to consider the cost of invested capital, both in terms of risk-free rate and risk premium. Therefore, maximizing earnings or return does not imply the maximization of shareholder value.

Maximizing earnings fails to account for the amount of capital invested to produce earnings. It could support the conclusion that any investment that produces earnings is convenient, no matter what return it earns or what risk it bears: in this case, a company would always prefer to retain and reinvest its earnings, rather than to pay them out to investors. Instead, it can be demonstrated that cutting the firm's dividends to increase investment will raise the stock price if, and only if, the new investment earns a rate of return on new investments greater than its cost of capital, i.e. the rate investors can expect to earn by investing in alternative, equally risky, securities.

When we use accounting rates of return like ROI or ROA, we risk to incur in the same problem. To illustrate, a manager that uses ROI in his/her investment decisions will be encouraged to select only projects that equal or exceed his/her SBU's or division's current ROI, no matter what is the value created by that investment in the longer term: projects of the same SBU or division can differ in risk and cost of capital from the average risk and cost of capital of the mix of assets in place. Obviously, these measures encourage managers to act much more in ways that are incongruent with the corporate objective of maximizing shareholder wealth, if they are measured and rewarded on maximizing them.

In marketing terms, it is imperative for businesses to allocate capital to endeavors that would be classified as "stars" in the Boston Consulting Group (BCG) matrix, and put to sleep those that would be classified as "dogs". Traditional accounting performance measures may not enable management to distinguish between these and in fact may encourage dogs to be fed more.

In order to avoid these misleading behaviors, hurdle rates or minimum acceptable rates for ROI are often based on an estimate of the business unit's (or division's) cost of capital. The essential problem with this approach is that ROI is an accounting measure of return, and cannot be compared to the cost of capital measure, which is an economic (or market) return demanded by investors.

We can demonstrate that the accounting return on investment differs from the economic return on investment as apples differ from oranges (the case of a single project can be easily extended to many projects):

- ACCOUNTING ONE-YEAR RETURN: (*cash flow* − depreciation − other non-cash charges + capital expenditures + incremental investments in working capital)/average (over the year) net book value (i.e. book value minus accumulated depreciation);
- ECONOMIC ONE-YEAR RETURN = (*cash flow* + change in present value)/ investment present value at the beginning of year. We can define the change of the present value over the year as *economic depreciation*. The economic return ($r$) can be derived as follows ($CF_t$ and $VA_t$ are cash flow and present value in year $t$, respectively):

$$VA_0 = \frac{CF_1}{(1+r)} + \frac{VA_1}{(1+r)}$$

$$VA_0(1+r) = CF_1 + VA_1$$

$$r = \frac{CF_1 + (VA_1 - VA_0)}{VA_0} = \frac{CF_1 + \Delta VA}{VA_0}$$

Note that, unlike economic income that depends strictly on cash flows, book income (the numerator of the accounting return) departs from cash flow since it does not incorporate the current year's investment outlays for working capital and/or fixed capital. In addition, non-cash items such as depreciation and provisions for deferred costs or losses are deducted in order to arrive at book income. Furthermore, depreciation represents the allocation of cost over the expected economic life of an asset. Accountants do not attempt, nor do they claim to estimate changes in present value. If depreciation and change in present value differ, then the book income will not be an accurate measure of the economic income.

Therefore, ROI is not an accurate or reliable estimate of the DCF return. Solomon (Solomon and Laya 1967) demonstrates that the extent to which ROI overstates the economic or DCF return is a complex function of the following factors (in parentheses the sign of the overstatement effect):

- length of project life (+)
- capitalization policy (−)
- speed of depreciation policy (+)
- time lag between outlays and their recovery by means of cash inflows (+)
- growth rate of new investments (−): if a company grows rapidly, its mix will be more heavily weighted towards new investments for which ROIs will be relatively low. Thus, the ROI of a growth company will be lower than that of a steady-state one, the investments' economic returns being equal. When growth rate and economic rate of return are equal, ROI equals them too. Thus, ROI differs from the economic return when the growth rate is greater or smaller than the latter.

**Table 1.1** The economic return of investing in a new restaurant

| | years (data in '000 €) | | | | |
|---|---|---|---|---|---|
| | **1** | **2** | **3** | **4** | **5** |
| Cash flows | 176.23 | 250 | 350 | 400 | 400 |
| Present value (15%) (at the beginning of year)[1] | 1000 | 973.76 | 869.80 | 650.28 | 347.84 |
| Present value (15%) (at the end of year) | 973.76 | 869.80 | 650.28 | 347.84 | 0 |
| Change in value (during year) (economic depreciation) | −26.24 | −103.95 | −219.52 | −302.44 | −347.84 |
| Economic income | 150 | 146 | 130.5 | 97.6 | 52.2 |
| Economic rate of return (%)[2] | **15** | **15** | **15** | **15** | **15** |

[1] The present value at the beginning of year is calculated by discounting the remaining cash flows at 15%

[2] The economic rate of return corresponds to the internal rate of return (IRR)

*source*: Rappaport (1986)

**Table 1.2** The ROI of investing in a new restaurant

| | years (data in '000 €) | | | | |
|---|---|---|---|---|---|
| | **1** | **2** | **3** | **4** | **5** |
| Cash flows | 176.23 | 250 | 350 | 400 | 400 |
| Depreciation (straight-line) | 200 | 200 | 200 | 200 | 200 |
| Accounting income | −23.77 | 50 | 150 | 200 | 200 |
| Net book value (at the beginning of year) | 1000 | 800 | 600 | 400 | 200 |
| Net book value (at the end of year) | 800 | 600 | 400 | 200 | 0 |
| Average book value | 900 | 700 | 500 | 300 | 100 |
| ROI (%) | **−2.6** | **7.1** | **30.0** | **66.7** | **200.0** |

*source*: Rappaport (1986)

Moreover, Solomon found that there is not a systematic pattern in the error that allows a correction to be made.

The following example (Tables 1.1, 1.2), referring to an investment in a new restaurant, shows that while the restaurant investment is expected to yield an economic return of 15%, the ROI figures are substantially different. ROI progresses from a negative figure in the first year to 200% in the fifth year, when the restaurant facilities are almost fully depreciated. Thus, ROI understates the economic rate of return in the first two years and significantly overstates it for the last three years. The five-year average ROI is approximately 23%, almost twice the 15% DCF rate of return. As this example illustrates, the accounting ROI typically understates the rates of return during the early stage of an investment and overstates them in later stages, as the asset base continues to decrease. Somebody might oppose that these errors offset one another over time, as the firm moves toward a balanced mix of old and new investments. Unfortunately, the errors are

**Table 1.3** The ROI in the steady-state

| | years (data in '000 €) | | | | | |
|---|---|---|---|---|---|---|
| | **1** | **2** | **3** | **4** | **5** | **Steady-state** |
| Accounting income (per restaurant) | | | | | | |
| 1 | −23.77 | 50 | 150 | 200 | 200 | – |
| 2 | | −23.77 | 50 | 150 | 200 | 200 |
| 3 | | | −23.77 | 50 | 150 | 200 |
| 4 | | | | −23.77 | 50 | 150 |
| 5 | | | | | −23.77 | 50 |
| 6 | | | | | | −23.77 |
| Accounting income (total) | −23.77 | 26.23 | 176.23 | 376.23 | 576.23 | 576.23 |
| Net book value (per restaurant) | | | | | | |
| 1 | 900 | 700 | 500 | 300 | 100 | |
| 2 | | 900 | 700 | 500 | 300 | 100 |
| 3 | | | 900 | 700 | 500 | 300 |
| 4 | | | | 900 | 700 | 500 |
| 5 | | | | | 900 | 700 |
| 6 | | | | | | 900 |
| Net book value (total) | 900 | 1600 | 2100 | 2400 | 2500 | 2500 |
| ROI for all restaurants (%) | **−2.6** | **−1.6** | **8.4** | **15.7** | **23.0** | **23.0** |

*source*: Rappaport (1986)

not offsetting. Table 1.3 illustrates this problem. One restaurant per year (the same investment discussed earlier) is opened during the first five years. Thus, from the fifth year the firm will find itself in a steady-state. The steady-state ROI is 23%, which significantly overstates the 15% economic rate of return.

In addition to the theoretical arguments, also the empirical evidence shows that the accounting information does not adequately explain, by itself, market valuations, nor it allows comparisons between firms: accounting data are therefore inadequate in reliably capturing a firm's true economic performance. Empirical data from many countries show the following evidence:

- no apparent relationship between EPS growth and total shareholder returns
- weak correlation between EPS growth and price/earnings ratio (P/E)
- robust correlation between market value and present value of expected cash flows
- statistically significant abnormal returns are observed when firms change the accounting approach to valuing inventories and computing the cost of sales: positive if they shift from FIFO to LIFO and negative in the opposite case. Therefore, if the inflation rate is non-null, market returns result to be influenced by the change in expected cash flows, while they do not react to changes in accounting methods: the shift from FIFO to LIFO, in fact, if the inflation rate is positive, reduces the accounting income and, other things equal, cash flows increase by means of smaller tax-payments

- greater correlation with market value added (market value of a company minus book value of its equity and debt) of the DCF performance measures, compared to that found with the accounting measures
- greater correlation with market value added of the residual income measures of performance, i.e. measures that account for the cost of capital invested.

## 1.4 Short Termism of Managerial Decision-Making

Accounting measures of performance can orientate management to a mistaken concern about maximizing the **current performance** measures. As anticipated above, a manager who is measured on maximizing ROI will be encouraged to select only projects that equal or exceed his/her division's current ROI, no matter what is the potential value of the investments in the longer term. Thus, the objective of maximizing ROI may prevent from approving projects that will create shareholders' wealth. Managers can maximize current profits by reducing discretionary expenses that may adversely affect future profitability by a reduction of future revenues (for example, R&D or other similar expenses like training and development, brand marketing, advertising, etc.) or an increase in future costs (for example, plant and machinery maintenance). These investments are characterized by taking a long time to translate initial outflows into financial results, and, as stated in most strategy textbooks, the long term survival of a firm is dependent indeed on this kind of investments.

In addition, ROI does not account for the post-planning period residual value of the business unit or company. Normally, only a small portion of a firm's market value depends on profits generated in a five-year span: the larger portion depends on cash flows generated beyond that point. A business attempting to increase its market share and competitive position will likely increase its new product development and marketing spending, price aggressively, and invest in expanded production capacity and working capital (Rappaport 1986). While these activities will strengthen the organization's long term strategic position and increase its market value, ROI is likely to decline over the coming several years. On the contrary, a harvesting strategy will generate better planning-period ROIs, but with an erosion of market share and a very small residual value.

## References

Graham JR, Harvey CR, Rajgopal S (2005) The economic implications of corporate financial reporting. J Acc Econ 40:3–73

Jensen MC (2004) Agency costs of overvalued equity. ECGI working paper series in finance 39

Rappaport A (1986) Creating shareholder value: a guide for managers and investors. Free Press, New York

Rappaport A (2005) The economics of short-term performance obsession. Fin Anal J 61:65–79
Solomon E, Laya JC (1967) Measurement of company profitability: some systematic errors in the accounting rate of return. In: Robichek AA (ed) Financial research and management decisions. Wiley, New York
Weissenrieder F (1998) Value based management: economic value added or cash value added? Gothenburg studies in financial economics 971214

# Chapter 2
# Competing Financial Performance Measures

**Abstract** The choice of financial performance measures is one of the most critical challenges facing organizations. Performance measurement systems play a key role in developing strategic plans, evaluating the achievement of organizational objectives, and rewarding managers. The measurement of financial performance in terms of accounting-based ratios has been viewed as inadequate, as firms began focusing on shareholder value as the primary long-term objective of the organization. Hence, value-based metrics were devised that explicitly incorporate the cost of capital into performance calculations. In this chapter, the following value-based measures are discussed, by focusing on their measurement logic: the economic value added (EVA), the cash flow return on investment (CFROI), the shareholder value added (SVA), the economic margin (EM) and the cash flow value added (CVA). The recently emerging emphasis on market value-based measures as the best metrics for value creation is also briefly analyzed.

**Keywords** Financial performance measures · Discount cash flow (DCF) model · Economic value added (EVA) · Cash flow return on investment (CFROI) · Shareholder value added (SVA) · Economic margin (EM) · Cash value added (CVA) · Residual income (RI) · Market value metrics

## 2.1 Trends in Performance Measurement

The choice of performance measures is one of the most critical challenges facing organizations. In fact, performance measurement systems play a key role in developing strategic plans, evaluating the achievement of firm's objectives and rewarding managers.

D. Venanzi, *Financial Performance Measures and Value Creation: The State of the Art*,
SpringerBriefs in Business, DOI: 10.1007/978-88-470-2451-9_2,

During the 1990s, many managers recognized that traditional accounting-based measurement systems no longer adequately fulfilled these functions.

A 1996 survey by the Institute of Management Accounting (IMA) found that only 15% of the respondents' measurement systems supported top management's business objectives well, while 43% were less than adequate or poor. Sixty per cent of the IMA respondents reported they were undertaking a major overhaul or planning to replace their performance measurement systems, in response to their flaws.

The perceived inadequacies in traditional accounting-based performance measures have motivated a variety of performance measurement innovations, ranging from "improved" financial metrics such as "economic value" measures to "balanced scorecards" of integrated financial and nonfinancial measures (Ittner and Larcker 1998). Despite most economic theories analyzing the choice of performance measures indicate that performance measurement and reward systems should incorporate any financial or nonfinancial measure that provides incremental information on managerial effort, firms traditionally have relied almost exclusively on financial measures such as profits, accounting and stock returns for measuring performance (Ittner and Larcker 1998). Schiemann and Associates conducted a U.S. survey of a cross section of 203 executives on the quality, uses and perceived importance of various financial and nonfinancial performance measures (Lingle and Schiemann 1996). Their results are summarized in Table 2.1. While 82% of the respondents valued financial information highly, more than 90% defined financial measures in each performance area, included these measures in regular management reviews, and linked compensation to financial performance. Conversely, 85% valued customer satisfaction information highly, but only 76% included satisfaction measures in management reviews, just 48% clearly defined customer satisfaction for each performance area or used these measures for driving organizational change, and only 37% linked compensation to customer satisfaction. Similar disparities exist for the other nonfinancial measures.

Most executives were weakly confident of any of these measures, with only 61% willing to bet their jobs on the quality of their financial performance information and only 41% on the quality of operating efficiency indicators, the highest rated nonfinancial measure (Ittner and Larcker 1998). In other words, there a wide gap exists between what is valued and what is considered accurate (Lingle and Schiemann 1996).

Nevertheless, it is interesting to note that this study supports the conclusion that good measurement is essential to good management (Lingle and Schiemann 1996).

In fact, partitioning the sample into two sub-samples[1]—measurement-managed and non-measurement-managed organizations—evidence emerges that the

[1] According to their reliance on measurement resulting from the survey: 58% of the organizations were identified as measurement-managed, as senior managers agree with measurable criteria for determining strategic success and management updated and reviewed semi-annual performance measures in at least three of the six types of performance areas.

**Table 2.1** Uses, quality and perceived importance of financial and non-financial performance measures

| | Type of performance measure | | | | | |
|---|---|---|---|---|---|---|
| | *Financial performance* | *Customer satisfaction* | *Operating efficiency* | *Employee performance* | *Community/ environment* | *Innovation/ change* |
| Information is highly valued[1] | 82% | 85% | 79% | 67% | 53% | 52% |
| Willing to bet job on the quality of the information[1] | 61 | 29 | 41 | 16 | 25 | 16 |
| Measures are clearly defined in each performance area[1] | 92 | 48 | 68 | 17 | 25 | 13 |
| Report measures are updated and reviewed at least seminannualy | 88 | 48 | 69 | 27 | 23 | 23 |
| Measures are included in regular management reviews[2] | 98 | 76 | 82 | 57 | 44 | 33 |
| Measures are used to drive organizational change[2] | 80 | 48 | 62 | 29 | 9 | 23 |
| Measures are linked to compensation[2] | 94 | 37 | 54 | 20 | 6 | 12 |

[1] per cent of executives responding to the survey who agreed with this statement
[2] per cent of respondents using these measures who agreed with this statement
*source*: ingle and Schiemann (1996)

measurement-managed organizations performed better than the non-measurement-managed counterparts on each of the following three performance measures:

- perceived industry-leadership over the past 3 years (74% vs. 44%);
- financial ranking in the industry top third (83% vs. 52%);
- success of the last major cultural and/or operational changes (97% vs. 55%).

Perceived inadequacies in traditional performance measurement systems as well as the managers' confidence in financial performance have led many organizations to place greater emphasis on "improved" financial measures that are claimed to overcome some of the limitations of traditional financial measures. We will review these "new metrics" in the following section.

However, more than 10 years later, this scenario seems to have changed only a little, paradoxically. Focusing on financial performance measures, international evidence indicates that managers remain anchored to traditional financial metrics. A recent survey of 400 U.S. financial executives[2] (Graham et al. 2005, 2006) shows that the vast majority view earnings—neither cash flows nor any of the "new metrics"—as the most important performance measure they report to outsiders. Nearly two-thirds of the respondents ranked earnings as the most important metric; fewer than 22% choose cash flows and less than 3% other metrics like the EVA. This obsession about earnings (i.e., EPS) was explained as follows (Graham et al. 2005):

- the world is complex and the number of available financial metrics is enormous. Investors need a simple metric that summarizes corporate performance, that is easy to understand and is relatively comparable across companies. EPS satisfies these criteria
- the EPS metric gets the broadest distribution and coverage by the media
- analysts assimilate all the available information and summarize it in one number, that is EPS
- analysts evaluate a firm's progress based on whether a company hits consensus EPS and investment banks assess analysts' performance by evaluating how closely they predict the firms' reported EPS.

The surveyed CFOs showed also a short term focus. Earnings benchmarks are quarterly earnings for the same quarter last year (85% of the surveyed CFOs agree or strongly agree that this metric is important) and the analyst consensus estimate for the current quarter (73.5%). The results strongly suggest that the dominant reasons for meeting or beating short-term earnings benchmarks relate to stock

[2] The empirical findings emerging from this survey are even more impressive because of the high representativeness of the sample: the companies range from small (15.1% of the sample firms have sales less than $ 100 million and 19% less than 500 employees) to very large (25% have sales of at least $ 5 billion and 35% more than 10,000 employees), they operate in many industries (manufacturing weighs 31%, but other sectors like retail, tech, transportation, banking, public utilities are represented) and cover a wide spectrum of ownership structures and CEO characteristics (age, tenure, education, insider ownership).

prices: more than 80% of the interviewed CFOs agreed that meeting benchmarks builds credibility with the capital market, helps maintaining or increasing the company's stock price, and conveys future growth prospects to investors. In other words, they believe that the price setters of their stocks (institutions and analysts, who are sophisticated investors) would not look beyond a short term earnings miss or irregularity in the earnings path.

Finally, they describe a trade-off between the short-term need to deliver earnings and the long-term objective of making value-maximizing investment decisions. Most of the surveyed CFOs would give up economic value in exchange for smooth earnings: they would decrease discretionary spending like R&D, advertising, or maintenance or delay starting a new projects in order to meet an earning target, even sacrificing value. In other words, they appear to be willing to burn "real" cash flows and not simply to rely on accounting manoeuvres for meeting accounting targets.

This traditional and apparently unchanged behavior in financial performance measurement seems to be confirmed by the empirical evidence that emerges from the most recent analysis about the most common financial metrics used in compensation plans, conducted in 2010 by the U.S. National Association of Corporate Directors (NACD) regarding about 1,300 individual from public company boardrooms across 24 industry sectors: profits and EPS (and similar ratios) weigh 97%, cash flow 36%, economic value measures like EVA and CFROI 16%, and stock price based measures 31% (multiple responses being allowed) (Daly 2011).

## 2.2 Economic Value Measures

### *2.2.1 The General Framework*

While traditional accounting measures such as earnings per share and return on investment are the most common performance measures, they have been criticized for not taking into consideration the cost of capital and for being too much influenced by external reporting rules.

While the traditional **discounted cash flow (DCF) model** provides for a complete analysis of all the different ways in which a firm can create value, it could become complex, as the number of inputs increases. Moreover, it could be very difficult to tie management compensation systems to a DCF model, since many of the inputs need to be estimated and could be manipulated to produce the desired results.

However, instead of an explicit DCF model, a simplified formula-based DCF approach could be used by making simplifying assumptions about a business and its cash flow stream, such as for example constant revenue growth and margins, so that the entire DCF can be captured in a concise formula (Copeland et al. 1990). The Miller-Modigliani (MM) formula (Exhibit 2.1), although simple, is a value of entity = value of assets in place + value of growth

$$\text{value of assets in place} = \frac{E(NOPAT)}{r}$$

$$\text{value of growth} = \sum_{t=0}^{\infty} I(t) \times \frac{r^*(t) - r}{kr}(1 + r)^{-(t+1)}$$

or simplifying,

$$\text{value of growth} = \mathrm{K}\,[\mathrm{E}(\mathrm{NOPAT})]\mathrm{N}\left[\frac{\mathrm{r}^* - \mathrm{r}}{\mathrm{r}(1+\mathrm{r})}\right]$$

where:

E(NOPAT)= expected net operating profit after taxes (assumed as proxy of expected cash flows after taxes)

r = cost of capital after taxes

I(t) = additional investments in period $t$ that will yield (starting in the period immediately following the investment) net profit at a constant rate $r^*(t)$

K = investment rate (% of cash flows invested in new projects)

N = intervals of competitive advantage

**Exhibit 2.1** The Miller-Modigliani DCF formula

particularly useful example for demonstrating the sources of a company's value (Miller and Modigliani 1961). The MM formula values a company as the sum of the value of the cash flow of its assets currently in place plus the value of its growth opportunities. This formula, although too simple for real problem solving, can be used to illustrate the key factors that will affect the value of the company, and therefore show how the two components of value performance can be measured separately.

In addition, it has been stated that the NPV concept is useful only if we can discount the investment's complete cash flow over its completed economic life: in other words, the cash flow approach becomes significant only when it is considered over the life of the business, and not in any given year. In practice, it could serve as a measure of performance only if it could be periodized into years, quarters, months or the time period of the user's choice. In fact, this is what some "new metrics" try to do.

If we assume that markets are efficient, we could replace the unobservable value from the DCF model with the **observed market price**, and reward or punish managers based upon the performance of the stock. Thus, a firm whose stock price has gone up is viewed as having created value, while one whose stock price goes down has destroyed value. Compensation systems based upon the stock prices, including stock grants and warrants, have become a standard component of most management compensation packages. While market prices have the advantage of being updated and observable, they are also noisy. Even if markets are efficient, stock prices tend to fluctuate around the true value, and markets sometimes do make big mistakes. Furthermore, a firm's stock performance seems to be much more reliable when evaluated over several years. Thus, a firm may see its stock price go up, and its top management rewarded, even as it destroys value. Conversely, the managers of a firm may be penalized as its stock price drops, even though they may have taken actions that increase firm value.

Summarizing, market value-based measures of performance can be affected by the following limitations:

- they reflect factors beyond managers' control, such as inflation and interest rates, for example. Actually, exogenous effects can be separated from the endogenous ones, but these corrections can be highly subjective
- they tend to aggregate relevant information in an inefficient manner for compensation purposes: their forward-looking character may result in compensating for promises and not for actual achievements
- they cannot be disaggregated beyond the firm level; thus, they cannot be used to evaluate the managers of individual divisions of a firm, and their relative performance; similarly they are not applicable to non-listed companies
- they can be influenced by investors' expectations which can be inconsistent with managers' rationale, because of the asymmetric information between investors and managers
- set as targets, they can increase the risk exposition of managers, distorting their risk perception when compared to the owners' risk perception; furthermore, managers should face the total risk and not only the systematic (or market) risk.

Nevertheless, a new emphasis on market value measure as the best metric for value creation is recently emerging. The Boston Consulting Group (BCG) remarks the following advantages of using **total shareholder return** (TSR) as the central metric of the entire corporate strategy process (Boston Consulting Group 2008):

- it incorporates the value of dividends and other cash pay-outs, which can represent anywhere from 20 to 40% (or even more) of a company's TSR;
- it integrates all the dimensions of the value creation system better than other accounting-based or cash-based metrics. We well know the pitfalls of accounting metrics. However, cash-based metrics by themselves could not capture the impact of improvements in the fundamental value on a company's valuation multiple or the full value of cash payments to investors. In fact, TSR performance can be broken down into the key drivers of value creation (as illustrated in Exhibit 2.2): (1) the growth of EBITDA (resulting from the combination of sales growth and change in margin) as an indicator of a company's improvement in fundamental value; (2) the change in the EBTDA multiple (the ratio of enterprise value—the market value of equity plus the market value of debt—to EBITDA) as a measure of how changes in investor expectation affect TSR; (3) the distribution of free cash flow to investors and debt holders (dividend yield, change in shares outstanding and net debt change) in order to measure the impact of paying out cash or raising new capital;

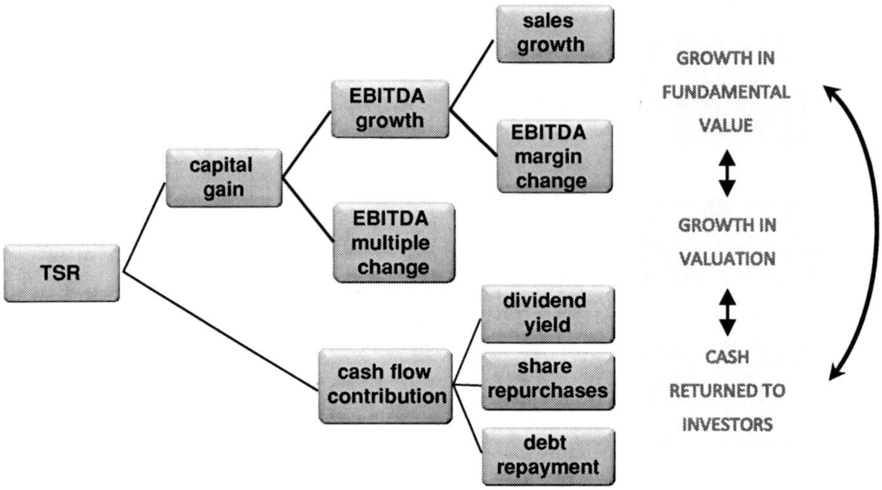


**Exhibit 2.2** Drivers of TSR
*source*: Boston Consulting Group (2008)

- the minimum appropriate TSR goal is easy to establish: it will be set by either the company's cost of equity or the expected average TSR of its peer group (assuming that this average is higher than the cost of equity). Therefore, the firm can easily state how much higher it should reach, depending on the aspirations of the senior team and on its competitive advantages and management capabilities.

Yearly, BCG elaborates global and industry rankings based on a 5-year TSR performance (www.bcg.com).

To counter the objection that the TSR could not be disaggregated beyond the firm level, BCG proposed the total business return (TBR) such as the internal mirror of actual external TSR, to which is highly correlated. TBR represents the intrinsic capital gain and dividend yield from a business plan, either at the corporate or the business unit level. It permits to cascade down the overall TSR value creation aspiration into internal corporate and business unit goals. It can work as a planning tool to assess the value creation potential of a business plan and help managers close the gap between aspirations and performance (Boston Consulting Group 2001), also driving in this context a portion of long-term incentives for business unit managers. The TBR results from the change in estimated equity value and from the equity free cash flows, which are the equivalents of the change in share price and dividends of the TSR, respectively.

Similarly, Stern Stewart & Co. (hereafter Stern Stewart) recently focuses their companies performance rankings on two metrics that use the TSR: the wealth added index (WAI) and the relative wealth added (RWA) (Stern Stewart 2002,

2003). Both are monetary amounts and are calculated by multiplying the TSR excess return by the initial market value of equity. The TSR excess return is calculated as the difference between the TSR and, respectively in the WAI and RWA calculations, the cost of equity and the peer TSR (i.e., the average TSR of a defined group of peers). These two measures should correct the main limits of TSR:

- they reflect the relationship between the money injected into a company and the resulting returns for shareholders
- they take into account the investors' required return
- they are cash figures and not percentages
- they reflect the risks taken by an investor in the form of the required return.

Previously, Stewart (Stewart 1991) proposed the **market value added** (MVA) as an appropriate market-based metric for ranking companies according to how much value they have added to (or subtracted from) their shareholders' investment. MVA is measured as the difference between a company's fair market value (of company' s total debt and equity capitalization) and the economic book value of capital employed in net assets. MVA should express the stock market's assessment of the net present value of all past and projected capital investments of a company: maximizing MVA should be the objective of any company that is concerned about maximizing its owners' wealth.

However, MVA appears inadequate to measure value creation (Weissenrieder 1998). In fact, shareholder's wealth is maximized by maximizing the difference between the firm's total value and the total capital that investors have committed to it, but we cannot define total capital as something derived from a company's balance sheet. The construction of the balance sheet is led by accountants and ruled by law, not by business reality or business logic. Firstly, the asset side of the balance sheet includes items such as non-strategic investments, prepaid expenses, inventories and supplies, etc. and it leaves out all strategic investments made in intangibles. Secondly, the time periods over which the assets are depreciated will not equal the actual economic life. Furthermore, these errors from the non-accounting point of view differ among both companies and lines of business. Finally, a company's balance sheet illustrates the capital base for the present value of the future cash flow from the business if no incremental strategic investments are made. The market value, by contrast, is the sum of the present value of the future cash flow from the business without any further strategic investment and the NPV of the cash flow from future strategic investments. Therefore, the MVA does not account for the value added of the business today but also includes the NPV of the company's future business (Weissenrieder 1998).

Consulting firms promoted a variety of "economic value" measures to overcome limitations of accounting-based and market-based measures. In this section the most known metrics are illustrated.

The more or less direct foundation for these *apparently new* performance measures is the concept of **residual income** (RI), developed many years ago (Worthington and West 2001). In the late nineteenth century Marshall stated that for investors to earn *true economic profit,* sales must be sufficient to cover all costs, including operating expenses and capital charges. Later, the desirability of quantifying economic profit as a measure of wealth creation was operationalized by Solomons (1965) as the difference between two quantities, net earnings and cost of capital. As early as in the 1920's General Motors applied this concept and in the 1950's General Electric labelled it "residual income", applying it as a performance measure to their decentralized divisions. RI is defined in terms of after-tax operating profits less a charge for invested capital, which reflects the firm's weighted average cost of capital. Close parallels are thereby found in the related (non-trademarked) concepts of abnormal earnings, excess earnings, excess income, excess realisable profits and super profits (Biddle et al. 1997). Economic profit (EP) is a variant of RI, but such as a return on equity. It is the book profit less the equity's book value (at the beginning of the considered period) multiplied by the required return to equity. As ROE is the ratio of profit after taxes to book value of equity, we can also express the economic profit as $EP_t = (ROE - k_e)Ebv_{t-1}$, where $Ebv_{t-1}$ is the initial book value of equity and $k_e$ is the cost of equity. It is obvious that for the equity market value to be higher than its book value, ROE must be greater than $k_e$, if ROE and are $k_e$ constant (Fernandez 2003).

## 2.2.2 Economic Value Added (EVA)

Stern Stewart's trademarked **economic value added** (EVA) is a proprietary adaptation of residual income. EVA is a modified version of residual income: the main modifications consist of accounting adjustments designed to convert accounting income and accounting capital to economic income and economic capital, respectively. Thus, the significance of the difference between EVA and residual income is dependent on the impact of these accounting adjustments.

EVA is determined as adjusted operating income minus a capital charge, and assumes that a manager's actions only add economic value when the resulting profits exceed the cost of capital.

$$\begin{aligned} EVA &= NOPAT - costofcapital \times capitalinvested \\ &= (ROIC - costofcapital) \times (capitalinvested) \end{aligned}$$

where

NOPAT = net operating profit after taxes

ROIC = return on invested capital = NOPAT/capital invested

According to EVA, the following strategies can be implemented to create value:

1. increasing EVA through improvements in ROIC (for example increasing asset turnover or repairing assets or structuring deals that require less capital);

2. investing in profitable growth, which means investing until ROIC exceeds the cost of capital;
3. reducing investments (and debts used to finance them) whose ROIC is less than the cost of capital (for example getting rid of unprofitable business);
4. increasing EVA by reducing the cost of capital, for example by designing capital structures that minimize the cost of capital.

We need three basic inputs for EVA's computation: the return on capital earned on an investment, the cost of capital for that investment and the capital invested in it.

We can estimate NOPAT in two ways (Damodaran 2000). One is to use the reported EBIT on the income statement and to adjust this number for taxes: NOPAT = EBIT (1− tax rate). When we use this computation, we ignore the tax benefit of interest expenses since it is already incorporated into the cost of capital (by an after-tax cost of debt). Alternatively, we can arrive at NOPAT by starting with net income as follows: NOPAT = net income + interest expenses (1− tax rate) – non-operating income (1− tax rate). Adding back the after-tax portion of interest expenses ensures that the tax benefit from debt does not get double counted.

It is more difficult to estimate the capital invested at the level of the firm than of a single project, because in a firm projects tend to be aggregated and expenses are allocated across them. One obvious solution may be to use the market value of the firm, but market value includes capital invested in assets in place as well as in expected future growth. If we want to evaluate the quality of assets in place, we need a measure of the market value of just these assets. Given the difficulty of estimating the market value of the assets in place, many analysts use the book value of capital as a proxy for the market value of capital invested in assets in place (Damodaran 2000). The "refined economic value added" (REVA), elaborated by Bacidore et al. (1997), calculates EVA applying the cost of capital to the opening market value (rather than book value) of the firm's equity plus debt.

We can measure invested capital in two ways. The *capital-based approach* considers the book values of equity and interest bearing debt (net of cash balances). The *asset-based approach* could arrive at a similar result using the book values of the assets of the firm as follows:

$$\begin{aligned} \textit{invested capital} &= \textit{net fixed asset} + \textit{current asset} - \textit{current liabilities} - \textit{cash} \\ &= \textit{net fixed asset} + \textit{non-cash working capital}. \end{aligned}$$

The two approaches could give non-equivalent results when the firm has long-term liabilities that are not interest bearing debt (for example personnel provisions and similar): they will be excluded from the invested capital computation when we use the capital approach. The reason we net out cash is consistent with the use of operating income as our measure of earnings. The interest income from cash or cash equivalents is not included in the operating income. Correspondingly, we have to consider the capital invested in operating assets only. In addition, the effects that dividends and stock buybacks have on returns can be viewed as an argument for using return on capital invested without cash balances. In fact, the return on equity of a firm that pays a large dividend or buys back stock will increase after the transaction because the book value of equity will decrease disproportionately, relative to the net income (in fact, the after-tax interest income earned on cash balances is generally smaller than the return on invested capital). This impact on book value of capital of stock buybacks is especially disproportionate when market value is significantly higher than the book value: in fact the book value of equity is reduced by the market value of the buyback; if the price to book ratio is for example 10, a buyback of 5% reduces the book value of equity by 50%.

However, it should be noted that, for companies with significant cash balances, the exclusion of cash from the invested capital and of its interest income from the NOPAT could make managers fail to use cash balances efficiently.

The book value, however, is a number that reflects not just the accounting choices made in the current period, but also the accounting decisions made over time on how to depreciate assets, value inventory and deal with acquisitions. In addition, it is influenced by the accounting classification of expenses into operating and capital expenditures, only the latter being part of the capital invested (Damodaran 2000). The limitations of book value as a measure of capital invested has led analysts who use EVA to adjust the book value of capital to get a better measure of capital invested.

Similar problems arise when we need to estimate NOPAT. The operating income that we would like to estimate would be the operating income generated by assets in place. The operating income, usually measured as earnings before interest and taxes in an income statement, may not be a good measure of this figure, for the same reasons that lead to adjust the book value of capital invested.

The practitioners who use EVA claim to make many adjustments to the accounting measures of both operating income and invested capital. Stern Stewart makes as many as 164 adjustments to arrive at EVA.

Exhibit 2.3 summarizes some of the adjustments recommended by Stern Stewart (Stewart 1991) for converting from book value and book NOPAT, on the one hand, to what it calls economic book value and economic NOPAT, on the other hand.

Some of these adjustments include (Damodaran 2000):

- **capitalizing any operating expense that will create income in future periods, although required to be expensed by accounting standards**. Some examples are: research and development (R&D) expenses, training and development, brand marketing, advertising, etc. The capital invested should be adjusted by capitalizing R&D expenses and augmenting by accrued R&D expenses, net of cumulative amortization. Correspondingly, the operating income should be considered without these expenses, but decreased by the annual amortization of these capitalized expenses. Making this adjustment for high-technology firms will drastically alter their return on capital, reducing it considerably in most

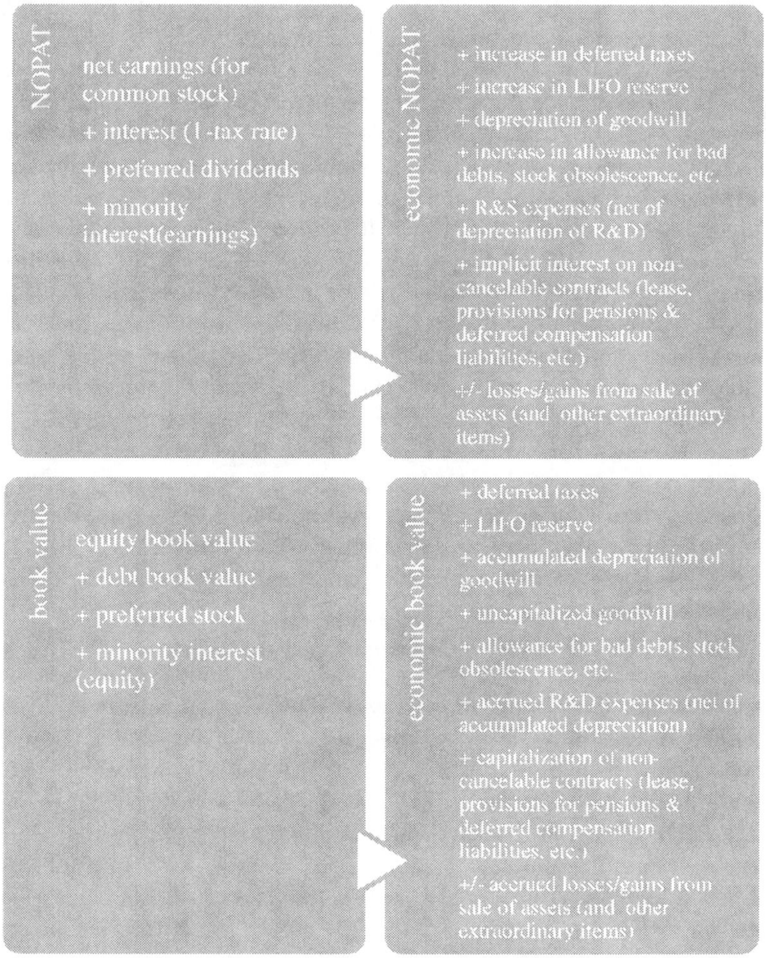


**Exhibit 2.3** Adjustments suggested by Stern Stewart for calculating the EVA

cases. Once you capitalize R&D, any new R&D increases this asset, but the existing R&D will be amortized over time, reducing it. The rate at which the R&D is amortized will be sector-specific and reflect the rate at which the benefits of new R&D decay in the sector;

- **capitalizing any operating expenses that mask financing expenses**. Common examples are lease expenses, which reduce the operating income in the period in which they are paid. From a financial standpoint, there is a little difference between operating and capital leases. Therefore, it does make sense to treat them homogeneously. Conversely, the accounting standards normally suggest adjusting for capital leasing but not for operating leasing. The standard adjustment operates as follows: the capital invested should be increased by the present value of the future lease commitments, which is treated as debt. On the contrary, the operating income should be decreased yearly only by the depreciation expense of leased asset and not by the entire lease payment. In fact, the interest portion of the lease payment is an interest expense and should affect the cost of capital. A similar adjustment regards provisions for pensions and other deferred compensation liabilities: they should be considered equivalent to debts and therefore included in the capital invested, and their implicit financial costs should be added back to NOPAT, since they should affect the cost of capital. For example, in Italy, "TFR" costs per year add up to 1.5% + 75% of inflation rate;

- **eliminating any items that modify the capital book value and the accounting earnings, without really impacting the invested capital and the economic income**. For example, the amortization of goodwill, that reduces the book value of capital but does not reduce the capital invested, should be added back; correspondingly, we should consider the earnings before amortization of goodwill. However, only the part of goodwill referred to the asset in place should be included in the invested capital: it can be measured as a difference between the acquisition price and the market value prior to acquisition.
  Other examples of this kind of correction are the following.
  Firstly, allowances for bad debts, stock obsolescence and similar items: they should be assimilated to equity reserves and therefore included in calculating the capital invested; correspondingly, changes (net of taxes) in these allowances should be added back to NOPAT. In this way, since these changes equal provisions less utilizations in the current year, NOPAT is affected only by the cash utilizations of this allowances, i.e. when the losses or the minor inflows occur. Secondly, the LIFO reserve. The LIFO reserve is the difference between the accounting cost of an inventory calculated using the FIFO method, and one using the LIFO method. In a typical inflationary environment, the value of a FIFO inventory is higher than the value of a LIFO inventory, so that the value of the LIFO reserve is : LIFO reserve = FIFO valuation—LIFO valuation. Since the reason for valuing an inventory using LIFO is usually to defer the payment of income taxes, the LIFO reserve essentially represents the amount by which an entity's taxable income has been deferred by using the LIFO method. The reserve should be added to invested capital and year-to-year increase to be added back to NOPAT.
  Thirdly, the one-time restructuring charges, which largely reduce the book value of capital. Assume, for example, a mediocre investment that earns only a 5% on continuing basis. However, let us assume that we write off half the investment, reducing the capital invested. Using the updated invested capital figure, the return on capital is now 10%, but the quality of the investment has not changed. To counter this, we should adjust the reported capital base for actions taken by the firm to reduce that base, but making this adjustment is much more difficult to do than adjusting earnings, since the effect on capital is cumulated (all restructuring charges, taken over time by the firm, affect the current capital invested). Similarly, we have to eliminate all the extraordinary items from the calculation of income and invested capital. As a general rule, we should

consider the earnings before any extraordinary item. For example, losses from sales of assets should be added back to net income, as well as gains should be subtracted. The capital invested should be adjusted similarly, in order to account for the actual impact of dismissals. For example, by adding back losses from sales of assets, we decrease the invested capital by the actual after-tax cash flow that would result from the asset sale. In fact, the book value would result decreased by the difference between the asset's original cost less the amount of accumulated depreciation. After such an adjustment, the economic value of the capital invested is just decreased by the asset's net liquidation value.

- **adjusting for any change in book value of capital that was hidden because of accounting treatment**. For example, when pooling is used to account for a merger, the book value remains in the balance sheet and the goodwill is ignored, i.e. is treated in the same way as an internally generated goodwill; therefore, the book value of capital should be corrected, augmenting it to reflect the price paid on the acquisition and the premium over book value. Note that the proportion of the premium paid for the expected future growth potential in the acquired firm should not be added on to arrive at capital invested since we need to estimate the capital invested in assets in place.

It is useful to reflect on the tax impact of making the above discussed adjustments. Generally speaking, if we add back to NOPAT the R&D costs previously expensed, we implicitly include the tax shield of these expenses in the NOPAT calculations. By contrast, if we add back the R&D expenses after taxes [i.e., the gross amount multiplied by (1 − tax rate)], we ignore it. Similarly, if we add back to NOPAT the R&D expenses minus the annual amortization of the capitalized R&D expenses, both after taxes, we are only considering the tax shield associated with the amortization.

The above are only some of the many suggested adjustments. Young and O'Byrne (2001) admit that *"....even the most ardent EVA advocate would concede that no company should make more than, say, 15 adjustments"*.

These authors further state that 10–12 accounting adjustments used to be most common, but that number has now declined to five or fewer, and in some case no adjustments are made. The explanations they give for this reduction are twofold: (a) managers are reluctant to deviate from GAAP-based numbers; (b) companies have found that most of the suggested adjustments have little impact on profit and capital.

Moreover, external analysts who choose to use EVA have to accept the reality that their estimates of operating income can be adjusted only for the variables on which there is public information.

Anderson et al. (2005) found that, in a sample of 317 USA firms over a 10 year time period, five accounting adjustments yielded on average an EVA only 7.1% lower than the EVA reported by Stern Stewart for the same firms and time period. The two accounting adjustments with the largest impact, the R&D and LIFO reserves, accounted for 92% of the total change in EVA due to the five accounting adjustments. The inconsistency over time of the differences, both in absolute and percentage terms, between Stern Stewart's EVA and Anderson et al.'s adjusted EVA, does not support the need for a large number of accounting adjustments. In addition, evidence shows a strong instability of the EVA adjustments over time and a very strong correlation between adjusted and unadjusted EVA. Therefore, accounting adjustments for EVA seem to be much to do about nothing.

The third and final component needed to estimate the economic value added is the cost of capital, which can be measured by the weighted average cost of capital. Stern Stewart suggests the use of the capital asset pricing model (CAPM) to estimate the cost of equity. A school of thought argues that in estimating the weighted average cost of capital the book value weights for debt and equity should be used, since both the return on capital and the capital invested are measured in book value terms. This argument does not really convince, for the following reasons (Damodaran 2000).

Firstly, we use the book value of capital for measuring the capital invested, but we want to estimate the market value of the assets in place. Therefore, using a book value cost of capital is essentially equivalent to assuming that all the debt is attributable to the assets in place, and that all the future growth comes from equity. It means that we would discount cash flows from the assets in place at the book cost of capital, and all cash flows from the expected future growth at the cost of equity.

Secondly, using a book value cost of capital for all the economic value added estimates, including the portion that comes from future growth, will destroy the basis of the approach, which is that maximizing the present value of economic value added over time is equivalent to maximizing firm's value.

Thirdly, being the capital structure a lever that increases EVA by decreasing the cost of capital, the market value cost of capital is more appropriate in this context, than the book value cost of capital.

Finally, from a practical view, using the book value cost of capital will tend to understate the cost of capital for most firms, and will understate it more for more highly levered firms than for less levered firms. Understating the cost of capital will lead to overstating the EVA. Thus, rankings based on the book value cost of capital are biased against firms with less leverage, and biased towards firms with high leverage.

### *2.2.3 Cash Flow Return on Investment (CFROI)*

A second economic value measure that has received considerable attention is the **cash flow return on investment** (CFROI) and its variants, proposed by HOLT Value Associates and Boston Consulting Group.

CFROI is essentially a modified version of internal rate of return (IRR), designed for investments that have already been made. The CFROI of a firm is compared to the cost of capital to evaluate whether a company's investments are good, neutral or poor. To enhance its value, then a firm should increase the spread between its CFROI and its cost of capital.

CFROI is calculated using **four inputs** (Damodaran 2000). The first input is the **gross investment** (GI) that the firm has in its assets in place. This is computed by adding back depreciation to the net asset value to arrive at an estimate of the original investment in the asset. In addition, non-debt liabilities (allowances) and intangibles such as goodwill should be subtracted. Finally, the gross investment is converted into a current dollar value to reflect the inflation that has occurred since the asset was purchased.

The second input is the **gross cash flow** (GCF) earned in the current year on that asset. This is usually defined as the sum of the after-tax operating income of a firm and the non-cash charges against earnings, such as depreciation and amortization. The operating income should be adjusted for operating (and capital) leases and any accounting effects, much in the same way that it was adjusted for in computing EVA (as well as GI).

The third input is the **expected life** of the assets in place ($n$), at the time of the original investment, which varies from industry to industry but reflects the earning life of the investments in question.

The expected value of the assets (the **salvage value = SV**) at the end of this life, in current dollars, is the final input. This is usually assumed to be the portion of the initial investment, such as land and buildings, that is not depreciable, adjusted to current dollar terms (practitioners include also inflation-adjusted current assets).

CFROI is the internal rate of return of these cash flows, i.e., the discount rate that makes the net present value of the gross cash flows and salvage value equal to the gross investment, and can thus be viewed as a composite internal rate of return, in real terms. This is compared to the firm's real cost of capital to evaluate whether the assets in place are value creating or value destroying. The real cost of capital can be estimated using the real costs of debt and equity and market value weights for debt and equity. However, according to the HOLT methodology (Credit Suisse-HOLT 2011), the firm-specific discount rate does not rely on the traditional CAPM-based estimates of the cost of capital, but is defined as a forward-looking discount rate, directly tied to the model's forecasting procedures for a firm's future cash flow stream[3] It is calculated in each country by observing market-implied discount rates across all companies in that country, which differ for two fundamental risk factors: liquidity risk (i.e., size risk differential) and credit risk (i.e., leverage risk differential). Hence, each company-specific discount rate is measured beginning with the country base (i.e., the discount rate for a standard company with a certain market capitalization and leverage) and adjusting it by market-specific differentials based on company-specific size and leverage. For all the European countries (excluding the UK), a Continental Europe base rate and Continental Europe differentials are used rather than country-specific base and differentials.

---

[3] A company-specific, market-implied discount rate is that rate which equates a company's forecasted net cash receipts to the company's current market value (Credit Suisse-HOLT 2011).

$$GI = GCFa_{n/CFROI} + \frac{SV}{(1 + CFROI)^n}$$

An alternative formulation of the CFROI allows for setting aside an annuity to cover the expected replacement cost of the asset at the end of the project life. This annuity is called the **economic depreciation** and it is computed as follows:

$$economic\,depreciation = \frac{replacement\,cost\,in\,current\,dollars}{((1+k)^n - 1)/k}$$

Where $n$ is the expected life of the asset, and the expected replacement cost of the asset is defined in current dollar terms to be the difference between the gross investment and the salvage value. The CFROI for a firm or a division can then be written as follows:

$$CFROI = (Gross\,Cash\,Flow - Economic\,Depreciation)\,/Gross\,Investment$$

The Appendix 1 shows the equivalence between the two formulas, when we assume, in deriving the economic depreciation, a discount rate $k = CFROI$. The differences in the discount rate assumptions account for the difference in CFROI estimated using the two methods above. In the first formula the intermediate cash flows are discounted at the CFROI, while in the second, at least the portion of the cash flows that are set aside for replacement, get reinvested at the cost of capital.

The IRR can be considered the basis for the CFROI approach. In investment analysis, the IRR on a project is computed using the initial investment on the project and all cash flows over the project's life. The IRR calculation can be done entirely in nominal terms, in which case the internal rate of return is a nominal IRR and is compared to the nominal cost of capital, or in real terms, in which case it is a real IRR and is compared to the real cost of capital.

At first sight, the CFROI seems to do the same thing. It uses the gross investment (in current dollars) in the project as the equivalent of the initial investment, assumes that the gross current-dollar cash flow is maintained over the project life and computes an internal rate of return. There are, however, some significant differences (Damodaran 2000):

- the IRR does not require the after-tax cash flows to be constant over a project's life, even in real terms, while the CFROI approach assumes that the real cash flows on assets do not increase over time. However, the CFROI formula can be modified to allow for real non-linear growth
- the second difference is that the IRR on a project or asset is based upon incremental cash flows in the future. It does not consider cash flows that have already occurred, which are considered as sunk. The CFROI, on the other hand, tries to reconstruct a project or asset, using both cash flows that have occurred already and cash flows that are yet to occur. The implications are relevant: a CFROI that exceeds the cost of capital is usually considered a sign that a firm is using its assets well, but this is not true when the IRR is less than the cost of capital.

From the CFROI we can derive the cash value added (CVA), by multiplying the spread between CFROI and cost of capital by the inflation-adjusted gross investment; or, alternatively, by subtracting from the gross cash flow both economic depreciation and capital charge. Note that this CVA figure differs from the indicator we will illustrate below. It can be considered a metric equivalent of CFROI but expressed in absolute terms; therefore, it can be easily compared to EVA, with respect to which it avoids some accounting distortions, particularly remarkable in capital intensive businesses.

### *2.2.4 Shareholder Value Added (SVA)*

The third economic measure is the **shareholder value added** (SVA) elaborated by Rappaport (1986) and LEK/Alcar Consulting Group and directly based on DCF logic. The key-factors in determining SVA are the following:

- growth rate of sales
- rate of operating profit margin (net of depreciation)
- (cash) tax rate
- rate of incremental fixed capital investment, in terms of rate of capital intensity of sales, net of depreciation (depreciation is implicitly considered equal to the replacement investment of fixed capital)
- rate of incremental working capital investment (in terms of rate of working capital intensity of sales)
- cost of capital, expressed in terms of weighted average cost of capital (WACC)
- value growth duration (planning period or competitive advantage period). It corresponds to the length of time during which the firm is expected to earn returns in excess of its cost of capital. It depends on how quickly company's strategies are more or less emulated by potential competitors.

These variables are combined in the following model in order to measure the value creation of a strategy (valid both in backward and forward-looking valuations):

*value created by strategy = change of shareholder value generated by strategy (with respect to non-strategy scenario)*

*shareholder value = gross corporate value – market value of debt and other obligations*

*gross corporate value = present value of operating cash flows (during the forecast period) + terminal value (at the end of the forecast period) + cash & cash equivalents and non-operating assets (whose returns are excluded from the operating cash flows)*

*operating cash flow*$_t$ = *sales*$_{t-1}$ × *(1+growth rate of sales)* × *rate of operating profit margin* × *(1- tax rate)* – *(sales*$_t$ – *sales*$_{t-1}$*)* × *rate of incremental investment in fixed assets and working capital.*

Cash flows and terminal value are discounted by the cost of capital.

The terminal value at the end of the forecast period can account for a great or small part of a company's (or business unit's) market value, depending on whether the firm is adopting a growth or an harvesting strategy.

The terminal value can be determined by using different approaches in different situations. It can be estimated as a liquidation value, when the firm ceases operations at the end of the forecast period, or as an equilibrium-state value of the ongoing firm, using a perpetuity of the net operating cash flow at the horizon, assuming a steady-state beyond this term or a constant rate of growth, continuing indefinitely. It should be observed that assuming a constant operating cash flow beyond the end of the forecast period does not imply a non-growth state of the business, but that the future new investments' rate of return is equal to their cost of capital; thus, incremental cash flows can be ignored in calculating the value of business. Alternatively, a multiple approach could be used.

While skewed versus future performance, SVA can measure historical performance periodically in terms of superior SVA, expressed as difference between actual and expected SVA, in a medium term span. This measure should correctly orient the operating managers to find strategies with the highest potential for increasing value, avoiding the short-term performance obsession.

### *2.2.5 Economic Margin (EM)*

The **economic margin** (EM) calculation is based on three components—operating cash flow, invested capital, and a capital charge—and is measured as follows:

$$EM = \frac{operating\,cash\,flow\ -\ capital\,charge}{invested\,capital}.$$

EM is considered by its advocates as a unique mixture of the two metrics EVA and CFROI, designed to capture the best qualities of each one (Obrycki and Resendes 2000).

The numerator of the EM is based, like EVA, on economic profit, which helps managers focusing on value creation. Furthermore, it shares with EVA the most common adjustments that clean up the accounting data. Unlike EVA, however, EM adds depreciation and amortization to determine cash flow, and instead explicitly incorporates the return of capital in the capital charge. Second, like CFROI, EM is based on inflation-adjusted gross assets, which helps to avoid the growth "disincentive" typically associated with net asset based measures. The capital charge is identical to a mortgage payment. The key difference between an EM capital charge and a mortgage payment is that when calculating a mortgage payment, the entire investment amount owed to the bank is treated as a depreciating asset. For most companies, however, part of their assets are non-depreciating (such as working capital) and can be returned to investors if the company is liquidated when its existing assets run out. Therefore, the capital charge is the annuity (at the cost of capital) that is due for the asset life in order to pay back the present value of the invested capital, net of the non-depreciating assets. The capital charge includes both the **return on capital** (the cost of capital rate on the initial invested capital) and the **return of capital** (the part of invested capital paid back each year).

Unlike CFROI, EM incorporates the investors required return on capital in its capital charge, and therefore it is a direct measure of shareholder wealth creation. A company with a positive EM should create wealth, a zero EM should maintain wealth, and a negative EM should destroy wealth. In addition, since the EM concept is derived from the economic profit, it is easier to communicate and set goals: for example, it is very easy to know the incremental cash flow required to obtain a 10% increase in the EM by multiplying EM by the per cent increase by gross investment.

## *2.2.6 Cash Value Added (CVA)*

The **cash value added** (CVA) is based on a net present value (NPV) model and periodizes the NPV calculation into years, months or the time period of the user's choice, and does not need to discount the investment's overall cash flows over its overall economic life (Weissenrieder 1998). It classifies investments in two categories, strategic and non-strategic, where the former (either in tangible or intangible assets) are investments whose objective is to create new value for shareholders, while the latter are investments made to maintain the value created by the strategic investments. Therefore, a strategic investment is followed by several non-strategic investments, which are considered as costs, while the business unit's capital base is the aggregate of every strategic investment's operating cash flow demand (OCFD). The OCFD is calculated as the cash flow, in real-term equal amounts every year, that, discounted using the appropriate cost of capital, will give the investment a null NPV over the strategic investment's economic life (it is a real annuity adjusted for actual annual inflation). The OCFD from each investment is the same in real terms every year, but it increases in nominal terms for two reasons: the inflation adjustment and, at an aggregate level, the new strategic investments. The CVA represents the value creation from the shareholders' standpoint, and can be expressed (by using yearly, monthly or quarterly data) as a difference between the operating cash flow (OCF) and the OCFD. OCF is measured as follows:

$$OCF = operating\,surplus$$
$$-\,working\,capital\,change - -non\,strategic\,investments$$

where operating surplus is equal to sales—costs (costs do not include depreciation and similar accounting items).

The CVA can be also expressed as an index (CVA index) if we calculate the ratio between OCF and OCFD (Weissenrieder 1998). In addition, in order to make explicit the main five value drivers (in relation to sales), we can express CVA as follows:

$$CVA = sales \times \left( \frac{operating\ surplus}{sales} - \frac{working\ capital\ movement}{sales} - \frac{non\ strategic\ investments}{sales} - \frac{OCFD}{sales} \right)$$

$$= sales \times \left( \begin{array}{c} operating\ surplus\ margin - WCM\ margin - \\ non\ strategic\ investments\ margin - OCFD\ margin \end{array} \right)$$

The CVA uses the same original figures as EVA, but the conclusion will be different. If we assume, for example, a ten-year steady growth scenario, that is expansion in identical investments with a positive NPV, the EVA of a single project is negative in the first years, but in the remaining years (until the end of the investment) it becomes increasingly positive. At the aggregate level, the growth will show poor profitability for a number of years, but profitability will boost after the expansion is stopped. It means that from the EVA's point view, the managers responsible for the expansion will be judged unprofitable, while the managers that stopped it probably will be judged very successful, and correspondingly rewarded if the bonus is based on the change in EVA from year to year.

By contrast, if we use the CVA approach, we have a CVA index stable for the entire considered period, at both the single and the aggregate investment level. Both OCF and OCFD, although equal in real terms, are increased by inflation, and the investment has the same profitability over time (if the investments create value, growth will be rewarded from the first year). At the aggregate level, both increase by inflation and by investment rate until the first investment run out, then they decrease with the running out-rate. Note that in a simplistic example, the NPV of the EVAs equals the NPV of the CVAs.

## References

Anderson AM, Bey RP, Weaver SC (2005) Economic value added adjustments: much to do about nothing? WP- Lehigh University

Bacidore MJ, Boquist AJ, Milbourn TT, Thakor AV (1997) The search for the best financial performance measure. Financ Anal J 53:11–20

Biddle GC, Bowen RM, Wallace JS (1997) Does EVA beat earnings? Evidence on associations with stock returns and firm values. J Account Econ 24:301–336

Boston Consulting Group (2008) Missing link–Focusing corporate strategy on value creation. The 2008 Value Creators Report

Boston Consulting Group (2001) Dealing with investors' expectations–a global study of company valuations and their strategic implications. The 2001 Value Creators Report

Credit Suisse-HOLT (2011) Credit suisse HOLT value search Reference handbook. wwwcredit-suissecom/holtemethodology

Copeland T, Koller T, Murrin J (1990) Measuring and managing the value of companies. ·McKinsey & Company Inc - Wiley, New York

Daly K (2011) Corporate performance metrics to top board agendas. Finan Exec 27(1):50–53

Damodaran A (2000) Value creation and enhancement: back to the future. Stern School of Business, New York

Graham JR, Harvey CR, Rajgopal S (2005) The economic implications of corporate financial reporting. J Account Econ 40:3–73

Graham JR, Harvey CR, Rajgopal S (2006) Value destruction and financial reporting decisions. Financ Anal J 62:27–39

Ittner CD, Larcker DF (1998) Innovations in performance measurement: trends and research implications. J Manag Account Res 10:205–238

Lingle JH, Schiemann WA (1996) From balanced scorecard to strategic gauges: is measurement worth it? Manag Rev 85:56–61

Miller MH, Modigliani F (1961) Dividend policy, growth and the valuation of shares. J Bus 34:411–433

Obrycki DJ, Resendes R (2000) Economic margin: the link between EVA and CFROI. In: Fabozzi FJ, Grant L (eds) Value-based metrics: foundations and practice. Wiley, New York

Rappaport A (1986) Creating shareholder value: a guide for managers and investors. Free Press, New York

Stern Stewart & Co (2002) Perspectives on business. Introduction to the wealth added index. Stern Stewart, Europe

Stern Stewart & Co (2003) Perspectives on business. Introduction to peer Relative Wealth Added. Stern Stewart Europe

Solomons D (1965) Divisional performance: measurement and control. Irwin, Homewood

Stewart GB (1991) The quest for value. Harper Business, New York

Fernandez P (2003) EVA economic profit and cash value added do NOT measure shareholder value creation. ICFAI J Appl Financ 9:74–94

Weissenrieder F (1998) Value based management: Economic value added or cash value added? Gothenburg studies in Financial Economics 971214

Worthington, Andrew, West, Tracey (2001) Economic Value-Added: A Review of theTheoretical and Empirical Literature. Asian Review of Accounting 9(1):67–86

Young SD, O'Byrne SF (2001) EVA and value based management, McGraw Hill, New York

# Chapter 3
# The Metrics War

**Abstract** Consulting firms have been battling for the last two decades over the superiority of their value metrics, charging that competitors' measures have flaws that compromise their evaluation ability. On the other hand, a growing number of firms have adopted various economic measures, moving from one metric to the other over the years, and often abandoning all of them in favor of traditional accounting measures. However, despite the increasing emphasis on these value measures, no definitive evidence exists of which metric works better than others, and research on the extent to which any of them is superior to the traditional accounting measures is limited and not yet univocal. In this chapter, we analyze the different economic value measures, by adopting different perspectives, from which their respective effectiveness can be evaluated: association with market financial performance, consistency with the discounted cash flow (DCF) approach in measuring value creation, and implications on managerial incentives. Metrics are compared from both a theoretical and an empirical standpoint, providing an updated synthesis of the main international evidence on their effectiveness.

**Keywords** Metrics war · Correlation between economic value measure and stock return · Firm value in terms of EVA and CFROI · Superior SVA for managerial compensation · Fade factor · Empirical evidence

## 3.1 Overstated Claims?

Considerable debate exists on the relative relevance of the alternative economic value measures. Consulting firms battle over the superiority of their economic value measures, charging that competitors' measures have flaws that compromise their evaluation and predictive ability.

D. Venanzi, *Financial Performance Measures and Value Creation: The State of the Art,* SpringerBriefs in Business, DOI: 10.1007/978-88-470-2451-9_3, 

A number of impressive claims have been made for each of the economic value measures.

Stern Stewart, for example, cites in-house research indicating that "*EVA stands well out from the crowd as the single best measure of wealth creation on a contemporaneous basis*" (Stewart 1991), while Dixon and Hedley (1993) of HOLT Value Associates cite an internal study showing that their CFROI measure explains 91% of the variation in market capitalization ratios.

Advocates of CFROI argue that this metric is vastly superior to traditional accounting measures, and EVA as a performance measure. In an article on the "metric wars" between consulting firms pushing various economic value measures, a partner at HOLT Value Associates claimed that "*CFROIs are ideally suited to displaying long-term track records, whereas a Stern Stewart-type EVA is in millions of dollars, heavily influenced by asset size, and unadjusted for inflation-induced biases*" (Myers 1996). Stern Stewart co-founder G. Bennet Stewart III responded: "*CFROI is literally a consultant's concoction. It was quite an imaginative development by a consulting firm, but it is not well grounded in the basic elements of corporate finance theory. CFROI attempts to measure shareholder wealth—which is not clearly related to maximizing shareholder wealth*" (Myers 1996).

The advocates of less known metrics like EM or CVA are less aggressive, but nevertheless assertive to point out the shortcomings of their better known competitors' metrics. Here is how the EM's inventors promote their metric: "*…sharing similarities individually with both EVA and CFROI, economic margin is a unique mixture of the two metrics designed to capture the best qualities of each measurement*" (Obrycki and Resendes 2000).

Weissenrieder (1998) replicates to the EVA advocates statement "*we keep it simple, EVA is all we need to know*" as follows: "*…it is simple because it is just like accounting, which is the framework we know today. Accounting is, however, what we now say we want to step away from. CVA is also simple but focuses on the relevant issues while EVA doesn't, and CVA is much more correct than EVA. We cannot be content with EVA if our ambition concerning the quality of information from our value based management process is high or if we have a high ambition on changing the organization towards understanding the meaning of the expression « shareholder value»*".

Claims such as these have caused a growing number of firms to adopt various forms of economic value measures. A 1996 survey by the Institute of Management Accountants (1996) found that 35% of the respondents used EVA or similar measures (up from 18% in 1995) and 45% expected to use them in the future (up from 27% in 1995).

Yet, despite the increasing emphasis on these measures, research on the extent to which they are superior to traditional accounting measures is not univocal. In the next sections we will analyze the different perspectives, with respect to which the various metrics' effectiveness should be evaluated.

## 3.2 The Association Between Economic Value Measures and Stock Returns

Many empirical studies have investigated the correlation of the most known value-based measures with excess returns, back-testing them against the underlying companies' actual wealth creation, as evidenced by subsequent stock price increases, or comparing them with MVA. Most studies to date have examined claims made by the proponents of each of these value-based measures that their own measures were better predictors of stock returns than traditional accounting measures or rival firms' measures. Since the declared goal of the new performance measures is to measure the increase in shareholder wealth, the correlation of such measures with stock returns has had an obvious appeal.

However, a strong statistical correlation with stock returns does not establish that a positive or an increasing value of a performance measure adds value. No measure of performance could ever have a higher statistical correlation with stock returns that the stock return itself. Thus, if this correlation were the only goal, firms should solely use performance measures based on changes in market value for compensation purposes and ignore all other measures. However, as mentioned above (see Sect. 2.2.1), stock returns can be a noisy and even misleading measure of managers' value added. Therefore, the rationale is that any financial measure used in assessing a firm's performance must be highly correlated with shareholders wealth, and on the other hand should not be subjected to the shortcomings of market-based measures.

This research domain includes studies which empirically investigate the degree of correlation between different performance measures (accounting- and value-based) and stock market returns and/or MVA. $R^2$ and regression models have been used to measure value relevance: in these regression models, total shareholder return or MVA (level or year-to-year change) are the dependent variables and the various performance measures (level or year-to-year change) are the explanatory variables. More recent studies noted that restricting the analysis to a single period contemporaneous association with firm values and returns does not address the problem that one-period measures of residual income are not necessarily associated with the shareholder changes in wealth reflected in security returns. Therefore, to face this problem, long-window methodologies are adopted (Forker and Powell 2008). Moreover, in order to take into account the impact on market value or total return of the difference between actual and expected performance measures, in some studies the dependent variable is expressed in terms of abnormal or unexpected returns and the competing performance measures (i.e. the independent variables) are measured in terms of levels and change specifications (Easton and Harris 1991) or, alternatively, of forecast errors, measured as the difference between the realized value of a performance measure and the market's expectation (Biddle et al. 1997). It is assumed that market expectations are formed according to a discrete linear stochastic process as a function of lagged observations of the performance measure. In some studies, the incremental information content of the economic measures is explored by introducing in the regression model the components in which the performance measure can be decomposed as explanatory variables; for example, in Biddle et al. (1997) EVA is decomposed in five parts: cash flow from operations, operating accruals, after-tax interest expense, capital charge, and accounting adjustments. In sum, researchers have employed two approaches, relative versus incremental information content, to compare the information usefulness of different measures. Relative information content evaluates which performance measure is superior in terms of association with stock returns, while incremental information content addresses whether one measure adds to the information provided by the other. The two approaches have different practical implications. Knowing the relative information usefulness, one will be able to choose a single best performance measure among competing ones. On the other hand, incremental information usefulness will help one decide whether to employ multiple measures in financial reporting. Both are important considerations in choosing performance measures. Frequently, an incremental approach is used by adding value-based measures to accounting counterparts in the regression model.

The empirical evidence about the association between the economic value metrics and the market-based performance measures is mixed and not definitive. Some studies reveal a stronger association of the economic value measures than the traditional accounting counterparts; by contrast, others report that the last are better predictors of stock returns than the former.

Some studies are concentrated on a specific economic measure (mostly EVA) compared to more traditional metrics; others compare the relative explanatory content of a larger set of metrics.

We will summarize below the main empirical findings.

Preliminarily, we point out that from the classic work of Hertz (1964), it has long been proved that any measure of value should consider the relevant cash flows over the appropriate time horizon. We avoid presenting here the vast majority of empirical studies which support the high correlation between market value or returns and DCF-based value or returns. Therefore, we will mainly focus on performance measures based on the residual income approach.

A first set of studies obtain empirical support to the claims that EVA is a better predictor of stock returns than traditional accounting measures.

- **Stewart** (1991) provided the first empirical evidence of EVA as a proxy for MVA. He reported a $R^2$ of 0.97 between changes in EVA and changes in MVA for 25 groups of firms over the period 1987–1988.
- **Milunovich and Tseui's** (1996) examination of the computer server industry found that the market-value added between 1990 and 1995 more highly correlated with EVA than with earnings per share, earnings per share growth, return on equity, free cash flow, or free cash flow growth.
- **Lehn and Makhija** (1997) also found that stock returns over a 10-year period were more highly correlated with average EVA over the period than with average ROA, ROS, or ROE. In addition, EVA performed somewhat better than accounting profits in predicting CEO turnover.

- **O'Byrne** (1996) examined the association between market value (in terms of MVA) and three performance measures: FCF (free cash flow), EVA and NOPAT. The sample included 9 years of data (1985–1993) of the companies in the 1993 Stern Stewart Performance 1000 (i.e. the MVA ranking of the 1000 largest publicly traded companies in the US, excluding financial institutions and public utilities). He found that EVA and NOPAT measures had similar explanatory power when no control variables were included in the regression models (about one-third); on the contrary, FCF resulted negatively correlated with the market value, and with null explanatory power (this evidence is not surprising since both poor performers and successful, but growing, companies are likely to have negative FCF). Furthermore, he verified that a modified EVA model (distinguishing between positive and negative EVA companies and considering capital multiples declining with company size) had greater explanatory power: the EVA model explains 56% of the market value variation with the industry specifications. In fact, investors are likely to capitalize positive EVA at more than its perpetuity value (a positive EVA company is able to earn more than its cost of capital and could be assumed to succeed in maintaining this rate of return); conversely, negative EVA should be valued at less than its perpetuity value, because investors presume that companies earning less than their cost of capital will not go forever without a turnaround that stops unprofitable investments. Moreover, as firms get larger, improvements in profitability become increasingly less likely; therefore, capital multiples tend to decline with company size. However, O'Byrne did not make similar adjustments to the NOPAT model, making it impossible to compare results using the two measures.

Other studies suggest that EVA is not the only performance measure that is directly tied to a stock's intrinsic value (one of the primary claims of EVA advocates); conversely, the competing metrics—both traditional and new—often outperform EVA.

- **Thomas** (1993) of BCG-HOLT, which advocate the competing metric CFROI, calculated a $R^2$ between MVA and EVA of just 4% for the 1,000 firms in the Stern Stewart database in 1988 (27% when extreme outliers are removed).
- **Chen and Dodd** (1997) examined the explanatory power of accounting measures (EPS, ROA and ROE), residual income, and various EVA-related measures. They found that EVA measures outperformed accounting earnings in explaining stock returns, but the associations were not as strong as suggested by EVA proponents (maximum $R^2 = 41.5\%$). In addition, accounting earnings provided significant incremental explanatory power above EVA, leading the authors to conclude that firms should not follow EVA advocates' prescription to completely replace traditional accounting measures with EVA. Finally, residual income provided nearly identical results as EVA, without the need for the accounting adjustments supported by Stern Stewart.
- **Biddle et al.** (1997) provide the most comprehensive study of EVA's value relevance to date. Their analyses examined the power of accounting measures

(earnings and operating profits) to explain stock market returns relative to EVA and five components of EVA (cash flow from operations, operating accruals, after-tax interest expense, capital charge, and accounting adjustments). They found that traditional accounting measures generally outperformed EVA in explaining stock price changes. While capital charges and Stern Stewart's adjustments for accounting "distortions" had some incremental explanatory power over traditional accounting measures, the contribution from these variables was not significant from an economic standpoint. Sensitivity analyses indicated that these results were robust to Stern Stewart's grouping of firms into five "types", based on their past operating returns and growth rates, the time period examined, and the dependent variable used in the tests (i.e. stock returns or absolute market value measures over different time periods).

- **Kramers and Peters** (2001) used the Stern Stewart 1000 database (the top 1,000 non-financial US firms, according to MVA) from 1978 to 1996 and measured the strength of the relation between EVA and MVA at industry level (53 industries according to Standard & Poor's industry classification codes). They regressed MVA on EVA and NOPAT for each firm $i$ over every year $t$ within each industry $j$ and they found that EVA is a superior proxy of MVA than NOPAT (i.e. $R^2_{MVA/EVA} > R^2_{MVA/NOPAT}$) only in 11 of the 53 industries. They controlled also for the capital intensity (FAT = fixed asset turnover) effect, because previous studies found that EVA is better suited to traditional manufacturing business than to knowledge-based ones, but they report that the ability of EVA to serve as proxy for MVA is not FAT-dependent. They obtained similar results when they regressed the changes in MVA instead of the levels of MVA, and also when the relationship between changes in MVA and changes in EVA and NOPAT was examined. In conclusion, they found: (1) no evidence supporting the conjecture that EVA is more suited for traditional manufacturing business with large amounts of tangible assets; (2) that NOPAT consistently outperformed EVA as a proxy of MVA.
- **Fernandez** (2003) analyzed 582 American companies using EVA, MVA, NOPAT and WACC data provided by Stern Stewart. For each of the 582 companies, he calculated the 10-year correlations between the yearly increase in the MVA and yearly EVA, NOPAT and WACC. For 296 companies (out of 582), the correlation between the increase in the yearly MVA and the NOPAT was greater than the correlation between the yearly increase in the MVA and the EVA. The NOPAT is a purely accounting parameter, while the EVA seeks to be a more precise indicator of the increase in MVA. There are 210 companies for which the correlation with EVA has been negative. The average correlation between the increase in MVA and EVA, NOPAT and WACC was 16, 21 and −21.4%, respectively. The average correlation between the increase in MVA and the increase of EVA, NOPAT and WACC was 18, 22.5 and −4.1%, respectively. He also found that the correlation between the shareholder return in 1994–1998 and the increase in CVA (the measure derived from CFROI) of the world's 100 most profitable companies was 1.7%.

- **Chari**(2009) presents a review of the empirical literature that evaluates the superiority of EVA over other traditional measures in terms of better association with shareholder's returns. He shows that the empirical findings are mixed. Only six out of the total ten studies examined (chosen by giving preference to differences in methodology, sample size and country of study) conclude that EVA is superior to other accounting measures; he attributes the inconsistency in the findings with respect to the superiority of EVA to the methodology and the impact of inflation. In fact, recent studies (Das et al. 2007) conclude that a non-linear S-shaped function better characterizes the return-earnings relationship; hence, the linear assumption can lead to the distortion of the findings in the related research. In addition, the discrepancy between accounting profits and true profits, along with inflation, distorts EVA (which is based on accounting profits).
- **Credit Suisse-HOLT** (2011)[1] present many examples of companies' wealth charts which show a straightforward correlation between CFROI dynamics over a 30-year period and total shareholder return relative to the relevant market index. Companies with high and improving CFROI levels, coupled with asset growth, present a rising trend in the TSR index; a deterioration in either the CFROI level or the asset growth performance is reflected in a poor company's performance relative to the market index. Growth associated with CFROI levels lower than the cost of capital does not create shareholder wealth; conversely, improved CFROI levels, coupled with no growth, generate a decreasing TSR index.

Finally, the following two studies faced a wider research question, i.e. whether residual income based measures perform better than measures which do not consider capital charge in forecasting stock return, obtaining partially contrasting evidence.

**Clinton and Chen** (1998) compared traditionally reported measures such as operating income, operating cash flow and ROI with new measures such as EVA, CFROI and Residual Cash Flow (RCF = operating cash flow − cost of capital × initial capital) in order to examine their correlation with stock prices and stock returns. The authors selected a sample of 325 firms from the Standard & Poor's 500 and the Stern Stewart 1996 Performance 1,000 databases, for the years from 1991 to 1995. They consistently defined all the items of the measurements in order to insure comparability and then conducted the correlation analysis between these measures and stock prices or stock returns. While residual-based measures have been heavily promoted as better choices than ROI-based measures, all three residual-based measures showed a lower association with stock values than their traditionally reported counterparts. Most of the RI and EVA correlations with stock prices or stock returns were either insignificant or of unexpected negative signs. Operating cash flow and adjusted operating income were the best-performing categories, and were better associated with stock price and stock return

[1] See for more details www.credit-suisse.com/holtemethodology.

compared to the other metrics. Of the three new measures, RCF is the only one that showed encouraging correlations. The more popular RI and ROI, and the most recently highly promoted EVA and CFROI, produced either insignificant or inconsistent correlations, and therefore indistinguishable in their relative lack of contribution to the assessment of firm value. The authors then suggest RCF as the best choice in linking profit to capital, and ultimately to market value. RCF maintains the advantages of using a cash-based and a residual-based measure. The residual cash flow measure is consistent with capital asset investment planning and already stated in terms of cash, so that adjustments to remove accounting distortions are not necessary.

More recently, **Forker and Powell** (2008) conducted a similar research, but reached different results. Comparing a larger set of metrics—NOPAT, pre-tax earnings (before and after extraordinary items), EVA, residual income variants (using different definition of capital base), and operating cash flows—they use a hindsight approach over a long-term horizon with two different samples: 3-, 5- and 10-year windows for a period of 16 years (1986–2001) and 12 years (1990–2001) on UK and US firms, respectively, provided by the Stern Stewart data-sets (the top 1,000 US firms and 500 UK firms, based on MVA, measured in 2001). The quality of the financial performance metrics is measured in terms of valuation errors, calculated as a difference between ex ante actual market value and ex post discounted metrics (means and standard deviations of valuation errors are analyzed): the smaller the mean and variability of the valuation errors, the higher are the accounting quality and the decision usefulness in forecasting future values of each metric, because the metric-specific realizations better reflect the accounting data on which investors build their expectations, in setting security prices. In addition, for any given window, the starting (*ex ante*) and terminal MVA for each firm are held constant across metrics in order to control for systematic market errors. In this way, the cross-sectional variation in the evaluation errors is attributable to valuation differences between metrics. However, it should be noted that the valuation errors reflect not only the quality of the metric, but also the easiness of forecastnig it. In summary, the main findings are twofold:

- all the residual-based metrics have lower and less volatile valuation errors than the other metrics; the differences among them are small and statistically insignificant, i.e. EVA does not outperform other RI metrics; by contrast, for the US sample, there is evidence that RI, using a conventional accounting definition of capital employed, is superior to EVA for longer windows
- cash flows from operating activities perform poorly compared to any RI-based measures: this finding can be consistent with the view that cash flows are relatively more difficult to predict, hence the higher valuation errors. These results could be also explained by the omission of the terminal value, that can weigh heavily in shorter windows.

In conclusion, from the above evidence, no certain and univocal conclusions can be drawn about the relative ability of different economic value measures to predict stock returns.

However, as widely observed (Damodaran 2000; Copeland 2002; Copeland and Dolgoff 2006), and from a theoretical standpoint, we would not expect any correlation between the performance measure levels and stock returns, or even between the change in performance measures and stock returns. This is because the market value is built on the expectations of future levels of performance measure. For example, whether a firm's market value increases or decreases on the announcement of a higher EVA, will depend on what the expected change in EVA was. For mature firms, for which the market might have expected no increase or even a decrease in EVA, the announcement of an increase will be good news and cause the market value to increase. For firms that are perceived to have good growth opportunities and were expected to report an increase in EVA, the market value will decline if the announced increase in EVA does not measure up to expectations. This phenomenon was recognized in relation to EPS for decades; the earnings announcements of firms are judged against expectations, and the surprise about earnings is what drives prices. The same apparent paradox can be generalized to CFROI and the other economic value measures. There is a relationship between CFROI and market value, with firms with high CFROI generally having high market value. For investors, however, the changes in market value are those that create returns, not the market value per se. Since market values reflect expectations, there is no reason to believe that firms with a high CFROI will earn excess returns. In fact, to the extent that any increase in CFROI is viewed as a positive surprise, firms with the largest increases in CFROI should earn excess returns. However, the actual change in CFROI has to be measured against expectations; if CFROI increases, but less than expected, the market value should drop; if CFROI drops but less than expected, the market value should increase. In summary, stock prices reflect investors' expectations about the future cash flows that a firm can deliver. If expectations are suddenly revised downward, the stock price will fall, even though earnings and return on capital are high.

In order to better show this phenomenon, **Copeland and Dolgoff** (2006) studied the empirical relationship between a measure of TSR (adjusted for general market movements) and various measures of firm performance, some of them expressed as absolute measures (EPS, EPS growth, EVA and EVA growth, all divided by the beginning-of-period price per share so that all the variables are expressed in percentages) and others (mainly earnings) as relative measure, i.e. changes in expectations (changes during the year in expectations about the same year's earnings, the following year's earnings and earnings three to five years beyond out[2]) for the S&P 500 firms during a 7-year period (1992–1998).

The following results emerged:

- a very weak relationship between the absolute performance measures and shareholder returns (with $R^2$s never exceeding 6%)

---

[2] Analyst expectations are used because they are considered a good proxy for the expectations of investors and management.

- a very strong relationship between the annual return to shareholders and changes in expectations (with $R^2 = 47\%$). Therefore, changes in expectations explain close to half of the company returns to shareholders. In addition, the results show that changes in expectations about the current earnings have an insignificant effect on the related year's shareholders return; conversely, a change in expectations about next year's earnings is statistically significant; however, the coefficient of changes of expectations about the long-term earnings growth is eight to ten times larger than that. Moreover, over the whole sample, the expected earnings for current and next years are strongly correlated (80%), but both have a relatively low correlation with the earnings growth expectations for the subsequent 3 to 5 years (about 30%): this evidence indicates that the long-term earnings expectations tend to contain different information
- unexpected increases in the cost of capital are associated with lower returns to shareholders.

These findings show that the difference between actual and expected performance takes on added significance. Therefore, we should define some metrics, both for analysing securities (externally) as for providing incentives and compensation to managers (internally), that measure financial performance relative to expectations.

Copeland and Dolgoff (2006) introduced expectations-based-management (EBM), which breaks down the economic profit—for example, in terms of EVA, the economic profit (EP) can be defined as ROIC minus WACC times invested capital (I)—into the differences between actual and expected performance of the three generic value drivers (ROIC, WACC, and invested capital) as follows:

$$
\begin{aligned}
EBM &= actual\ EP - expected\ \mathrm{Ep} = (\mathrm{actual\ ROIC} - \mathrm{expected\ ROIC}) \times \mathrm{I} \\
&\quad + (actual\ WACC - expected\ WACC) \times I + (ROIC - WACC) \\
&\quad \times (actual\ I - expected\ I).
\end{aligned}
$$

The first term says that we can create value by earning more than expected on the existing invested capital; the second term says that we can create value by reducing the cost of capital by more than expected; the last term says that the growth resulting from (unexpected) new investment adds value only if the new investment earns more than its cost of capital.

According to the EVA's logic, EBM can be defined as $\Delta$EVA − expected EVA improvement (EI) (O'Byrne and Young 2006).

In conclusion, shareholder value creation (driven by changes in expectations) may not be correlated with economic value creation (which is created when the cash flows are realized) in the short run; over the long run they must be correlated, because in the long run investors will adjust their expectations to the reality of the level of cash flows being realized (Copeland and Dolgoff 2006).

## 3.3 The Association Between Economic Value Measures and DCF

In the following sections we will illustrate how to reconcile the EVA and CFROI (and, consequently, EM) approaches with the DCF model, while we omit the consideration of SVA and CVA, which are directly and explicitly consistent with the DCF framework.

Therefore, as we will analytically show below, through the present value of EVA and CFROI we can obtain the same firm value as with the discounting of cash flows, using the well-known DCF approach. That means that it is possible to value firms by discounting EVA or CFROI, although these parameters do not represent cash flows and their financial meaning is much less clear than that of cash flows. Therefore, we will conclude that maximizing the present value of EVA or CFROI is equivalent to maximizing the value of the firm.

However, as widely observed (Damodaran 2000; Fernandez 2002), maximizing a particular year's EVA or CFROI (and EM) is meaningless: it may be the opposite of maximizing the value of the firm. The claim that EVA, CFROI or EM measure the firm's "value creation" in each period is a tremendous error.

As we will better show below, the firm's value depends on the present value of all the expected streams of EVA, from the asset in place and from future investments, as well as on the initial capital invested. Similarly, the firm's value, while a function of CFROI, is also a function of the other variables in the equation, i.e. the gross investment, the tax rate, the growth rate, the cost of capital and the firm's reinvestment needs.

**EVA and DCF**

The equivalence between a project's present value of the EVAs over its life and its NPV has been widely demonstrated (Damodaran 2000; Dillon and Owers 1997; Jackson 1996).

The NPV of a project can be written as follows:

$$NPV = \sum_{t=1}^{t=n} \frac{EBIT_t(1-t) + DEPR_t}{(1+k)^t} + \frac{SV_n}{(1+k)^n} - I$$

where

$DEPR$ = depreciation and amortization
$SV_n$ = salvage value
$k$ = cost of capital
$I$ = initial investment
$n$ = expected life of the investment

Now we can express the initial investment $I$ as follows:

$$I = \sum_{t=1}^{t=n} \frac{k(I)}{(1+k)^t} + \frac{I}{(1+k)^n}$$

and substituting this expression into the first equation, the NPV of the original project is the following:

$$NPV = \sum_{t=1}^{t=n} \frac{EBIT_t(1-t) + DEPR_t}{(1+k)^t} + \frac{SV_n}{(1+k)^n} - \sum_{t=1}^{t=n} \frac{k(I)}{(1+k)^t} - \frac{I}{(1+k)^n}$$

Now, if we assume that the project has a salvage value of zero, and that the present value of depreciation is equal to the present value of the initial investment, discounted back over the project life, we can write the NPV of this project as follows:

$$NPV = \sum_{t=1}^{t=n} \frac{EBIT_t(1-t)}{(1+k)^t} - \sum_{t=1}^{t=n} \frac{k(I)}{(1+k)^t}$$

which can be reconciled with the present value of the EVAs

$$NPV = \sum_{t=1}^{t=n} \frac{EVA_t}{(1+k)^t}$$

Thus, the NPV of the project is the present value of its EVAs by that project over its life.

Note, however, that this reconciliation formula holds only when the assumptions above are verified. In other words, only if the cash flows from depreciation are really the capital being returned to the firm, which means that we are considering an annuity depreciation method. More generally, we can eliminate the hypothesis of a salvage value of zero and we can assume that the cash flows from depreciation pay back $I - SV_n$.

The link between EVA and NPV allows us to express the value of a firm through the EVA (Damodaran 2000; O'Byrne 1996). The firm's value can be expressed in terms of value of the assets in place (aip) and of the expected future growth (fi = future investments), as follows (see Exhibit 2.1):

$$\text{firm value} = \text{value of assets in place} + \text{value of expected future growth}$$

Note that in a DCF model, the values of both the assets in place and the expected future growth can be written in terms of net present value created by each of them:

$$\text{firm value} = \text{capital invested}_{\text{aip}} + \text{NPV}_{\text{aip}} + \sum_{t=1}^{t=\infty} \text{NPV}_{t,\text{fi}}$$

Substituting the EVA version of NPV into this equation, we have:

$$\text{firm value} = \text{capital invested}_{\text{aip}} + \sum_{t=1}^{t=\infty} \frac{\text{EVA}_{t,\text{aip}}}{(1+k)^t} + \sum_{t=1}^{t=\infty} \frac{\text{EVA}_{t,\text{fi}}}{(1+k)^t}$$

Thus, the value of a firm can be written as the sum of three components: the capital invested in the assets in place, the present value of the EVAs by these assets, and the expected present value of the economic value that will be added by future investments. Thus, a policy of maximizing the present value of EVAs over time is equivalent to a policy of maximizing the firm's value. However, the notion that the EVA approach requires less information than a DCF valuation, or that it provides a better estimate of value is false. The EVA approach, if correctly applied, should obtain the same value as a DCF valuation, and requires more information, not less, because it needs an additional input, i.e. the capital invested in the firm. It uses this measure to break down the firm's value into capital invested and EVA components. Note that changing the amount of capital invested has no impact on the overall value, because if it increases, the present value of EVAs from the assets in place proportionally decreases (Damodaran 2000). Finally, it is often affirmed that the EVA approach provides us with new insights on value creation because it emphasizes the excess return: it can be easily observed that a DCF model in which growth is linked to the reinvestment rate and to the return on investments (see the M&M formula in Exhibit 2.1) achieves the same objectives and reaches the same results.

We can re-write the previous formula using the Stern Stewart's terminology as follows:

$$\text{firm value} = \text{current operations value (COV)} + \text{future growth value (FGV)}$$

where COV measures the value of the business "as is", without any expectation of improvements in operating margins or new capital investment. The firm's value can be expressed as follows: $\text{COV}_0 = \text{cap}_0$ (book value at the end of year 0) + capitalized current EVA ($EVA_0/k$). The FGV measures the spread between the expected return on new capital investment and the cost of capital ($k$) multiplied by the present value of future capital investment: it can be expressed as the capitalized present value of future annual EVA improvements ($\Delta EVA_i$) with respect to the current EVA, as follows:

$$FGV_0 = (1+k)/k \times \sum_{i=1}^{\infty} \frac{\Delta EVA_i}{(1+k)^i}$$

Obviously, the firm value can depend in different ways on COV and FGV. For example, the COV portion of market value tends to be very high in mature markets such as food processing and tobacco, and relatively low in growth markets such as technology.

This approach in expressing the firm's value permits us to complete what we discussed at the end of the previous section, when we described the EBM approach. In fact, as O'Byrne and Young (2006) affirm, we can use FGV for deriving the expected improvements in EVA (or EI, as defined under Sect. 3.2) that is reflected in the firm's current market value. If its value can be expressed as the sum of COV and FGV, we can consider that investors want a cost-of-capital return on the market value of their investment, which means a cost-of-capital return on both COV and FGV. The company's NOPAT, with no EVA improvements, will provide only a cost-of-capital return on its COV; in fact, we have:

$$k \times COV_0 = \left(cap_0 + \frac{EVA_0}{k}\right) = k \times cap_0 + EVA_0$$
$$= k \times cap_0 + NOPAT_0 - k \times cap_0 = NOPAT_0$$

Therefore, the company's return on its FGV ($k \times FGV_0$) must come from an increase in either the current EVA or in the expected future EVAs which corresponds to an increase in FGV. Therefore, the following relationship holds:

$$k \times FGV = \Delta EVA/k + \Delta EVA + \Delta FGV.$$

In order to derive EI (i.e. the expected EVA improvement which is implicitly assumed by the investors in the current market value) we need a formula that shows how changes in EVA are expected to be related to changes in FGV. In other words, we need a coefficient $\alpha$ such that $\Delta FGV = \alpha \times \Delta EVA/k$. Therefore, we can derive EI, implicit in current market value of the firm:

$$\Delta EVA = EI = \frac{k \times FGV_0}{\frac{1+k+\alpha}{k}}.$$

We can put $\alpha = 0$, which implies that every euro (or dollar) of increased EVA translates into $(1 + k)/k$ of additional COV without causing any change in FGV.

Alternatively, we can derive $\alpha$ by the following formula, if we assume that the capital growth rate (g), the ROIC and the cost of capital are all constant:

$$\alpha = \frac{(1 + WACC) \times g}{WACC - g} - 1$$

More realistically, we can estimate $\alpha$ empirically, from a regression analysis of ΔFGV as a function of ΔEVA.

Therefore, as discussed above, an EBM approach in designing a compensation plan in terms of EVA implies that the bonus earned should be anchored to a certain percentage of the (ΔEVA − EI) spread.

In conclusion, in order to address the point discussed at the end of the previous section (Sect. 3.2) using this framework, it can be observed that a regression analysis, which tries to explain the excess investor return in terms of EVA improvements, would need two explanatory variables (in a generic year $n$): (1) the capitalized future value of the excess EVA improvements for years 1 through $n$; (2) the excess FGV at the end of year $n$ (O'Byrne 1997). In fact, it could be demonstrated (see Appendix 2) that the excess investor return in year $n$ can be expressed in terms of EVA as follows:

$$\left(\frac{1+k}{k}\right)\sum_{i=1}^{n}(EVA_i - EVA_{i-1})(1+k)^{n-i}$$
$$+\left(\frac{1+k}{k}\right)\sum_{i=n+1}^{\infty}\frac{x_n\Delta EVA_i - x_0\Delta EVA_{i-1}}{(1+k)^{i-n}}$$

where $x_n \Delta EVA_i$ measures the investor's expectation, at the end of year $n$, of the EVA improvement in year $i$.

**CFROI and DCF**

The link between CFROI and firm value can be showed starting from a simple discounted cash flow (DCF) model for a firm in a state of stable growth (Damodaran 2000):

$$\textit{firm value} = FCFF_1/(k - g_n)$$

This can be rewritten in terms of CFROI as follows:

$$\textit{firm value} = [(CFROI \times GI - DA)(1 - t) - (CX - DA) - \Delta WC]/(k - g_n)$$

where

$FCFF$ = free cash flow to firm = EBIT(1 − t)−(Capital Expenditures − Depreciation) − Change in Working Capital
$CFROI$ = cash flow return on investment
$GI$ = gross investment
$CFROI \times GI$ = economic income
$DA$ = depreciation and amortization
$CX$ = capital expenditures
$\Delta WC$ = change in working capital
$k$ = cost of capital
$g_n$ = stable growth rate.

It should be noted that the firm's value, while a function of CFROI, is also a function of the other variables in the equation, i.e. the gross investment, the tax rate, the growth rate, the cost of capital, and the firm's reinvestment needs.

A more sophisticated formulation recognizes the fact that value comes from the CFROI not just on the assets in place but also on the future investments; thus we can express the value of the firm as a sum of the following terms:

- the present value of the cash flows from the assets over their remaining life, which can be written as $\sum_{t=1}^{t=n} \frac{CFROI_{aip} * GI_{aip}}{(1+k)^t}$ where $CFROI_{aip}$ is the CFROI on the assets in place, $GI_{aip}$ is the gross investment in the same assets and $k$ is the real cost of capital
- the present value of the excess cash flows from future investments, which can be written in real terms as $\sum_{t=1}^{t=\infty} \frac{CFROI_{t,fi} * \Delta GI_t}{(1+k)^t} - \Delta GI_t$, where $CFROI_{t,fi}$ is coming from future investments made in year $t$, and $\Delta GI_t$ is the new investment made in year $t$. Note that if $CFROI_{t,fi} = k$, this present value is equal to zero.

The key to avoiding a perpetuity assumption is to determine when a company's return on capital is equal to its cost of capital (i.e. the discount rate). Afterward, no matter how much a firm grows, the net present value of future investments is zero and therefore they can be ignored.

HOLT addresses this point allowing for a **fade factor** in CFROI, meaning that the current CFROI fades towards the real cost of capital over time. In general, a company's current value depends on competitive life-cycle patterns that reflect expected future economic returns and reinvestment rates (Madden 2007). The idea of competitive life-cycles is based on the premise that competition and capital flows operate over the longer term to force companies' economic returns toward the cost of capital. During the high innovation stage, returns are above their cost of capital and reinvestments exceed internally generated funds. Attracted by the wealth creation opportunities, competitors attempt to replicate innovations. Competition results in a tendency of economic returns to fade towards the long term average of the industry's corporate economic returns, which approximates the industry's corporate long term cost of capital (moving the cost of capital towards this long-term average return, too). Thus, corporate reinvestment rates fall back towards the lower, long term average growth rate of the overall economy. To maintain well-above-average economic returns and reinvestment rates over decades, companies must continually reinvent themselves in order to outperform competitors.

The fade factor can be estimated empirically by looking at firms in different CFROI classes and tracking them over time (Credit Suisse-HOLT 2011). HOLT's research has shown that the persistence of the company's CFROI level can be determined as a function of the following factors: CFROI level used in valuation, CFROI level volatility, reinvestment rate and company's future real asset growth rate. From such an analysis, for example, it emerges that high CFROI level companies, with stable returns and low growth, fade at a slower rate than high CFROI level companies with volatile returns and high growth. Big winners and losers in the market are those companies that deviate from the expected life-cycle fade factor.

A long-term fade horizon of 100 years is used (although a smaller 40-year window is generally enough): the assumption is that after 100 years the CFROI levels will have faded (up or down) to the long term average of 6%, growth will have faded (up or down) to the long-term average of 2.5% and the firm-specific discount rate will have faded to 6% (i.e. equal to the CFROI). The fade factor is expressed as the percentage of the CFROI level spread above or below the long-term average that is expected to dissipate by the end of a 5-year fade window, assuming a constant exponential rate of dissipation during the period. For example, if the t + 1 CFROI level is 10% and the fade factor is 25, the t + 5 forecasted CFROI level, assuming a long-term average rate of return of 6%, will be $10 - [0.25 \times (10 - 6)] = 9\%$. From the end of the fade window until year t + 100, a constant exponential final fade rate of 10% per year is assumed.

Some companies appear able to better withstand the competition pressure, showing highly persistent CFROI levels that fade more slowly than those of an average firm. Less than 10% of firms within the HOLT database exhibit this persistence: they are dominated by companies with large market capitalizations and strong brand names. The following threshold tests for identifying these companies are empirically derived: (1) CFROI level above 8% for a minimum of five consecutive years; (2) excess returns decrease no more than 10% per year; (3) CFROI level volatility below 30% per year; (4) asset growth rate below 30% per year.

In conclusion, we can summarize that a firm's value will depend upon the CFROI it earns on the assets in place and on both the **abruptness** and **speed** with which this CFROI fades towards the cost of capital. Thus, a firm can potentially increase its value by doing any of the following, other things being equal:

- increase the CFROI from the assets in place, for a given gross investment
- reduce the speed at which the CFROI fades towards the real cost of capital
- reduce the abruptness with which CFROI fades towards the cost of capital.

Note that this approach does not differ from an analysis of the firm's value in the DCF format: cash flows from the assets in place are related to the current CFROI; the length of the high growth period can be linked to the fade speed, and the growth rate during the growth period implies how sharply the excess returns fall (Damodaran 2000).

**EM and DCF**

Being the EM framework a mix of EVA and CFROI, its reconciliation with the DCF approach can be made straightforwardly from the previous formulas. Like in EVA, the EM's numerator is the economic profit. In addition, similarly to the CFROI valuation model which considers the fade factor, the EM framework adopts a concept called decay. The key difference between decay and fade is that instead of decaying returns, the EM framework decays economic profits to zero over time.

Decay is defined as the yearly percent of EM that is lost due to competition. The EM approach utilizes decay rates derived from empirical research that relates EM level, EM variability, EM trend and firm size to the decay rate. In general, the more positive and variable the EM and the smaller the invested capital, the higher the decay.

In fact, firms with very high (positive) EMs face stronger competition than firms with EMs near zero. Second, if a firm has had a very unstable EM pattern, the investor will tend to assume that the extreme (positive or negative) values will not persist for very long and will assign the firm a high decay rate. Conversely, if the company has a very steady EM history, the investor is more likely to believe that management can maintain this EM level over a longer period, and will assign it a low decay rate. Finally, larger firms have lower decay rates than smaller firms, because they are more able to defend their competitive advantage (for example by means of barriers to entry that enhance profitability or large fixed costs that are hard to restructure in difficult times).

Therefore, given an initial EM level, and investment, a discount and decay rate, a future investment as well as an existing asset may be evaluated. The EM approach values existing assets similar to future investments, except that it adds back the capital charge to the economic profits to obtain the cash flow from the existing assets. Since the existing assets have already been purchased, the initial investment is a sunk cost and only the cash flow from the investment is relevant.

The present value of the capital charge exactly equals the investment, and that is why the EM approach reconciles itself with the DCF framework: hence, the discounted value of the economic profits on future investments provides the correct NPV. Moreover, when EM equals zero, the contribution of any future investments to value is zero, and the perpetuity problem associated with the typical DCF forecasts would be eliminated.

EM's advocates (Obrycki and Resendes 2000) claim that the decay construct (very similar indeed to the fade factor), by fading economic profits, avoids the need to force all companies to the same "fade to level" which characterizes the CFROI framework. Hence, the EM approach would eliminate separate "fading paths" for the cost of capital and return rates, which could produce value destroying behaviors.

## 3.4 Managerial Implications of the Economic Value Measures

From a managerial standpoint, the key question is not whether the economic value measures are more highly correlated with stock returns than traditional accounting measures, but whether the use of economic value measures for internal decision-making, performance measurement, and compensation purposes, improves organizational performance (Ittner and Larcker 1998).

According to Rappaport (1986), we can summarize as follows the main criteria a performance metric should satisfy in order to correctly support compensation plans:

- being consistent with the main value drivers
- being verifiable (in order to limit manipulation)
- being dependent on levers that managers can influence or control
- being clear and easily communicable.

Before debating whether the companies have in fact gained value by adopting the economic value measures, it is worth noting the way in which these measures have been put into practice.

Since EVA is the most popular measure of performance and has widespread application across industries and continents, in over the last two decades we have seen many corporations converting to EVA. Most firms that have adopted EVA as their value enhancement measure have also tied management compensation to it. Some firms have made it the sole basis for compensation, while others continue to use it in association with other compensation schemes. The adopters of EVA still measure it looking at year to year changes rather than in terms of the present value of EVAs over time. The reward may be simply based upon achieving an EVA in the coming year that is greater than the current year's figure. In other firms, managers are rewarded only if they beat the expected EVA. In almost no case is the reward based upon the present value of EVAs over time. This practice does create a significant potential for abuse, as we will see below. Firms that have converted to EVA have

**Table 3.1** Uses of economic value (EV) measures in business planning and incentives plan (survey of 114 firms by Sibson & Co. 1995)

| | |
|---|---|
| **EV used in business planning/financial management**[1] | **41.2%** |
| **EV used as a performance measure in incentive plans** | **16.7%** |
| **If EV is used in incentive plans**: | |
| Used in annual incentive plans only | 42.1 |
| Used in long-term incentive plans only | 10.5 |
| Used in annual and long-term incentive plans | 47.4 |
| Used in corporate and business unit management plans only | 52.6 |
| Used in corporate management plans only | 5.3 |
| Used in business unit management plans only | 31.6 |
| Used in corporate, business unit, and small group plans | 10.5 |
| EV is the sole performance measure in incentive plans | 26.3 |
| Effectiveness of EV as a measure in the incentive plan: | |
| Very successful | 26.3 |
| Moderately successful | 36.8 |
| Not successful | 0.0 |
| Not sure | 31.5 |
| No response | 5.3 |

[1] The survey defined EV as cash flow earnings above the cost of capital or DCF, including measures such as EVA, CFROI, EP, and RI
*source*: Ittner and Larcker (1998)

done so not just at the firm level, but also at the level of individual divisions or sub-units within the firm. Thus, the success or failure of an employee is often measured by the EVA of the unit to which this employee is most closely connected. This practice greatly emphasizes the estimation problems about EVA (Damodaran 2000). Similar practices should be supposed in relation to CFROI.

A 1995 survey by Sibson & Co. supports claims that many users of the economic value measures do not base compensation on these measures (see Table 3.1): while 41.2% of respondents used economic value measures (e.g. measures such as EVA, CFROI, residual income, etc.) for business planning and financial management purposes, only 16.7% used these measures in incentive plans, and only 26.3% of these made economic value the sole performance measure in their plans. In addition, many of the respondents used economic value measures only in annual incentive plans and not in long-term plans, and relatively few used them at all the organizational levels.

We can deduct that criticism persists about the current compensation systems, if we consider that: (1) a commission of 30 experts from the boardroom, the C-suite, the investment world and major business professions have convened at NACD (i.e. the 2010 NACD Blue Ribbon Commission on performance metrics) to tackle the issue of properly matching executive compensation to performance; (2) among the six recommendations (to guide boards in setting the performance metrics used by their companies) made by the commission, on the basis of the observed practices among US companies (Daly 2011), the following poit out the difficulty of selecting appropriate metrics and implementing them in effective reward systems:

- establish company performance metrics to cascade throughout the entire enterprise
- track company performance against metrics on an on-going basis
- reward executives based on performance as measured by appropriate metrics.

Let us therefore analyze some distortions that can arise from using EVA or CFROI in compensation plans.

Assume that a firm adopts EVA and decides to judge managers based upon their ability to generate greater-than-expected EVA (Damodaran 2000).

Let us go back to the equation in which the firm's value is decomposed into capital invested, the present value of EVA by the assets in place and the present value of EVA by the future growth.

$$\text{firm value} = \text{capital invested}_{\text{aip}} + \sum_{t=1}^{t=\infty} \frac{\text{EVA}_{t,\text{aip}}}{(1+k)^t} + \sum_{t=1}^{t=\infty} \frac{\text{EVA}_{t,\text{aip}}}{(1+k)^t}$$

The first two terms in the equation (i.e. the capital invested and the present value of EVA by these investments), are both sensitive to how the capital invested is measured. If the invested capital is reduced, keeping the operating income constant, the first term in the equation will drop, but the present value of EVAs will increase proportionately. Hence, when managers are judged based upon the EVA, they will have a strong incentive to keep the invested capital down. Thus, if the reduction in the invested capital comes from closing down a plant that does not (and is not expected to) generate any operating income, the cash flow generated by liquidating the plant's assets will increase value. However, if the reduction has purely cosmetic effects on the invested capital, it does not create and may even destroy value. Some examples are: (1) accounting changes that reduce the book value of capital, but do not generate tax benefits or higher operating income in future periods (for example, large one-time restructuring charges); (2) playing games once the rules for the EVA measure have been defined (incentive to lease rather than buying assets).

Furthermore, the value of a firm is the value of its assets in place and that of its future growth prospects. When managers are judged on the basis of EVA in the current year, or of year-to-year changes, the EVA that is being measured is just that from the assets in place. Thus, managers may willingly sacrifice long-term competitiveness (the EVA from future growth) in the interest of pursuing short-term targets (higher EVA from the assets in place). In addition, EVA's present value is a function of both the EVA and the cost of capital. A firm can take actions that increase its EVA, but still end up with a lower value, if these actions increase its operating risk and thus the cost of capital. When managers are judged based upon year-to-year EVA changes, they will tend to shift investments into riskier investments. This tendency will be overstated if the cost of capital does not reflect the changes in risk or lags it, for example when beta estimates, that are based upon historical returns, defer changes in risk.

The relationship between CFROI and firm value is less intuitive than the relationship between EVA and firm value, partly because CFROI is a rate of return. Nevertheless, the games that managers can play, when their performance is judged on the basis of CFROI, are similar to those noted in discussing EVA.

The first is the capital game, when the CFROI is increased while the gross investment is reduced: since value is driven by their product, a firm could increase CFROI and end up with a lower value. Thus, managers of firms judged on the basis of CFROI will do everything in their power to keep the gross investment as small as possible.

CFROI, even more than EVA, is focused on the assets in place and does not look at future growth. To the extent to which managers increase CFROI at the expense of future growth, the value can decrease while the CFROI goes up. This is because the effects of the growth sacrifice are likely to be observed in the fade factor, and unless this can be precisely estimated and compared to what it should have been, managers will continue to play the growth game (Damodaran 2000).

Although the CFROI is compared to the cost of capital in order to judge whether a firm is creating or destroying value, it represents only a partial correction for risk. The value of a firm is still the present value of the expected future cash flows. Thus, a firm can increase its spread between the CFROI and the cost of capital, but still end up losing value if the present value effect of having a higher cost of capital dominates the higher CFROI. In general, then, an increase in CFROI, by itself, does not indicate that the firm value has increased, since this might have come at the expense of lower growth and/or higher risk.

What about SVA? Since the focus of SVA is future performance, it seems difficult to apply it when measuring historic performance. However, superior SVA as a difference between actual and expected SVA, in a medium term span, should correctly orient the operating managers to find strategies with the highest potential for increasing value, avoiding the short-term performance obsession. Rappaport (1999) explains the superior SVA approach for an incentive pay plan of operating managers at business units' level (that is, an intermediate level between the CEO/corporate level executives and frontline managers). SVA puts value on changes in the future cash flows of a company or business unit. According to SVA approach, business unit's managers should be rewarded when they create superior SVA in their units. According to Rappaport (1999), calculating superior SVA requires six steps:

- first, develop expectations for the main drivers of value (sales growth, operating margins and investments) by considering historical performance, the unit's business plan, and competitive benchmarks
- second, convert the value drivers expectations into annual cash-flow estimates and discount them at the business unit's cost of capital in order to obtain the value of each business unit
- third, aggregate the values of each business unit to verify that the sum approximates the company's market value
- fourth, fix the annual expected SVA over 3 years on the basis of the cash flows used to value the business unit

- fifth, use year-end results to compute the actual SVA at the end of each year (the same as in the previous step but with actual figures instead of estimates)
- sixth, the difference between actual and expected SVA, if positive, measures the superior SVA.

Since value creation prospects can vary greatly from one business unit to another, an approach based on expectations permits to account for differences in business prospects. Managers who perform extraordinarily well in low return businesses will be rewarded, while those who do poorly in high-return businesses will be penalized: setting the SVA threshold targets at 80% of a designated target would be appropriate. In addition, it should be noted that value creation is a long-term phenomenon: therefore, annual performance measures do not account for the longer-term consequences of operating and investment decisions made today. To motivate managers to focus on opportunities to create superior SVA beyond the current period, the performance evaluation period should be extended at least to a rolling 3-year cycle.

We will examine now some empirical evidence about the effects on managerial behavior induced by the adoption of the economic value measures.

**Wallace** (1997) examined the relative performance changes in 40 adopters of residual income-based measures such as EVA, EP and CVA (derived from CFROI) and a matched sample of non-users. Compared to the control firms, the residual income firms decreased new investments (−21%), increased payouts to shareholders through share repurchases (+112%), sold (or withdrew) 100% more assets and utilized assets more intensively, leading to significantly greater change in residual income. These actions result to be consistent with the strong rate of return discipline associated with the explicit capital charge in residual income-based measures. Wallace also found weak evidence that stock market participants responded favorably to the adoption of residual income-based compensation plans.

**Kleiman** (1999) compared the performance of 71 companies that adopted EVA between 1987 and 1996 with that of their most direct competitors that did not adopt the EVA. He demonstrated that the adoption of EVA-based performance evaluation system resulted in substantial improvements in EBITDA and operating margins, faster asset turns and stronger cash flow generation, which are in turn the drivers of the superior stock market performance of the corresponding companies. Sale of assets increases significantly after the introduction of EVA, too. Thus, the adoption of EVA led to substantial internal improvements, which resulted in higher shareholder returns than those of the direct competitors: 2.6% in the year of introduction, and 5.7, −1 and 11.1% during the subsequent years.

**Balachandran** (2006) criticized Wallace's and Kleiman's results because they presumed that firms implementing residual income-based measures in compensation plans switched from earnings-based plans, therefore hypothesizing that investments should decrease because, given the incentives to maximize earnings, managers would choose all the investments which earn a return higher than the firm's cost of debt. Conversely, he examined whether the investments differ for firms switching to RI-based compensation from earnings or ROI-based compensation plans. In fact, given the incentives to maximize ROI, managers will choose projects which earn a ROI at least equal to the prior firm's average ROI and therefore, if the latter is higher than the cost of capital, a firm that switches from ROI to RI can invest more under RI than under ROI. Balachandran identified a sample of 147 firms and partitioned it further in two subsamples, respectively those switching from ROI- and those switching from earnings-based compensation plans. The empirical results can be summarized as follows: (1) in the pooled sample there is no evidence of changes in investment being associated with the adoption of RI, but a significant increase in delivered RI as predicted; (2) there is a significant and positive difference in investment between the firms switching from ROI and those switching from earnings. Conversely, the predicted changes in investment before and after RI—negative in the "earnings" subsample and positive in the "ROI" subsample—are neither univocally significant nor robust.

**Hogan and Lewis** (2005) analyzed the effects of adopting economic profit plans (EPPs)—in the 9-year window around the adoption year—in investment behavior, operating performance and change in shareholder value of a sample of 108 firms during the 1983–1996 period. Economic profit plan are defined as systems that reward managers if earnings exceed a charge for the use of the capital employed in the business. Various are the economic performance measures included in selecting the sample: EVA, RI or EP. For investment policy, three variables were considered: new investments, asset disposals and acquisitions, all of which scaled by total assets. EEPs provide incentives to managers to invest in positive NPV projects. Thus, asset disposals are expected to increase following an EPP adoption. The prediction for new investments and changes in acquisition activity is less clear: to the extent that some firms overinvest in negative NPV projects that generate accounting profit, new investments should decrease; however, if firms underinvest in positive NPV projects that have relatively low profitability rates, the EPP adoptions could increase new investment. Analogously, the predicted sign for changes in acquisition activity is indeterminate. Operating performance is analyzed in terms of economic profits, accounting rates of profitability, and the use of assets-in-place. Top-level operating performance is measured in terms of economic profits, EBITDA and net income, all scaled by total assets. Then the three measures of operating performance are also scaled by total sales for breaking down the operating performance into components, and calculating three measures of asset turnover (for analyzing asset utilization): asset turnover, accounts receivable turnover and inventory turnover. All the margin measures and all of the turnover measures are expected to increase following an EPP adoption. However, improvements are expected to be greatest for the economic profit margins and smallest for the profit margins. Finally, changes in shareholder value following the adoption of an EPP are examined using the market-to-book ratio, that is expected to increase following an adoption if the performance improvements are expected to be permanent.

The main empirical results can be summarized as follows:

- asset sales increase in the post adoption period, new investments significantly decrease but there is no significant change in acquisition activity
- top-level operating performance generally improves after the adoption; the ratio of economic profits to assets shows significant improvement in two of the four post-adoption years, while the economic profit margin is insignificant: this suggests that improvements in economic profits are caused by capital management decisions rather than by improvements in margins
- both total asset turnover inventory turnover increase significantly in the post-adoption period
- finally, the median adopter's market-to-book ratio increases from the year preceding the adoption until the fourth year after adoption, suggesting that the market anticipates positive effects from EPP adoptions and investors believe that the changes are permanent.

However, these improvements resulted similar to those realized by a set of non-adopting control firms. The possibility that some firms are better candidates for an economic profit plan than others was then considered, and adopters were classified according to whether they made anticipated or surprising choices in adopting EPP. The study found that anticipated adopters made changes in investment behavior that reduced the invested capital and allowed them to become more profitable than a sample of control firms that were expected to adopt but continued using a traditional plan. This suggests that EPPs work best for firms that are expected to adopt such plans. This expectation is influenced by some pre-adoption firm-specific characteristics. For example, the growth opportunities and profitability: managers of with high growth opportunities but relatively low income levels from assets-in-place will prefer a value-based compensation because the opportunity to receive an earning bonus is scarce; conversely, managers of firms with relatively high accounting profitability would be content to continue a more traditional earnings-based plan. Similarly, both the investment policy and the ownership structure matter: firms with high capital expenditures encourage an EPP adoption because it creates incentives to select positive NPV projects and sell underperforming assets; if management's interests are already aligned with those of the shareholders (as a result of their share ownership), the firm may be less likely to adopt an EPP.

**Ryan and Trahan** (2007) examined the effects on performance of adopting value based management (VBM) systems in a sample of 84 firms (selected among the US 1,000 largest publicly owned industrial and non-financial services companies) during the period 1984–1997. The surveyed firms base compensation on VBM metrics and use VBM for evaluation, budgeting and monitoring. Four VBM metrics are adopted: SVA, CFROI, ROIC (compared to the cost of capital to evaluate performance) and RI measures like EVA. All these are single period measures of performance, take into account return on invested capital and the relevant cost of capital, and are all consistent with the DCF approach. The performance effect is measured in terms of change in residual income divided by invested capital or sales or assets, from pre-adoption year to until 5-years after the adoption. The results support the premise that VBM improves economic performance: the median change in relative RI divided by the invested capital ranges from a minimum 4.46 for the period −1 to +3 and a maximum 8.96 for the period −1 to +4; these changes are statistically significant. No one component of RI (NOPAT, invested capital, and the cost of capital) individually drives the results, but rather all the components appear to work together. Other empirical findings are the following:

- firms that base compensation on VBM do not appear to improve their performance better than those that do not use it. This result can be explained in terms of stronger obstacles that firms that tie compensation to VBM face for improving their economic performance: they use the VBM metric to provide incentives for managers;
- VBM is not more or less effective for high-growth firms than for low-growth firms. A VBM system could improve the performance more in growth-firms than in low-growth ones only if the system helps these firms at identifying value-creating investments; however, greater information asymmetries that characterize these firms can make it more difficult to design their corporate governance systems;
- the VBM's efficacy does not depend on the capital investment intensity: both groups of firms with capital expenditures above and below the sample median experience a performance improvement for all the post-adoption periods. Since VBM systems reward managers for the efficient allocation of the invested capital and penalize managers for overinvestment, we would expect that VMB could be more useful to high-capital-expenditure firms;
- similarly, the performance improvements are not significantly different for high-net-working-capital firms and low-net-working-capital firms. Two opposite reasons could potentially explain differences in performance improvement between the two sub-samples. Working capital is a non-budgetary item (it is not formally analyzed as are capital projects) and then it is often influenced by discretionary decisions: therefore, high-net-working-capital firms can better reduce that investment to improve the VBM performance metrics. In contrast, low-net-working-capital firms have fewer observable assets and VBM would generate additional information about managers' actions;
- no evidence emerges that any type of system (with respect to the metrics used in measuring performance) outperforms all the others;
- controlling for firm-specific factors, the stronger and more significant result is that large firms appear to be less successful than small firms in achieving benefits from adopting VBM systems. This is consistent with the consideration that larger firms face more complex and difficult implementations;
- finally, high-capital-expenditure firms are more likely to cut capital expenditures subsequent to the adoption of VBM systems: however, but the differences between high- and low-capital-expenditure firms are statistically significant for all the post-adoption periods except for period −1 to +1. Thus, no evidence

would support the premise that the single-period metric and the focus on invested capital could result in a myopic investment strategy in favor of a short-term performance improvement.

A related issue is whether the performance implications of the economic value measures depend on **how the measures are used** within the organization. Stern Stewart argues that an effective implementation of EVA requires firms to make this measure the cornerstone of a total financial management system that focuses on EVA for capital budgeting, goal setting, investor communication, and compensation (Stern et al. 1995). Stewart (1995) asserts that the poor results from many EVA implementations are attributable to the fact that its use has not become pervasive throughout the organization, especially for compensation decisions. He attributes the lack of success in many EVA implementations to four factors: (1) EVA is not made a way of life; (2) EVA is implemented too fast; (3) lack of conviction by the CEO or division head; (4) inadequate training. As reported in a Stern Stewart study (www.EVA.com) companies that implemented EVA in the 1990s outperformed their peers by an average of 8.3% per annum over the 5 years following the adoption and created total excess shareholder wealth of $ 116 billion. A more recent study of the performance of EVA companies, concentrating on the period since the peak of the stock market on March 2000 through midyear 2002, showed that the portfolio of Stern Stewart's EVA clients earned a total return of 36.5% and beat the S&P 500 by a total of 69.8%. The performance differential was even more significant for companies that reinforced EVA as a performance measure and decision tool by tying management incentives to it. These firms earned a 64.5% return, whereas companies that used EVA only for performance measurement earned a 20.2% and beat the market by 53.5%. The evidence seems to be consistent with the contention that EVA works best when it is used in a powerful bonus plan that stimulates ownership and directly aligns the interests of managers and employees with those of the owners. However, tests and data are provided by Stern Stewart, that are strongly interested in suggesting the most pervasive use of EVA.

**Biddle et al.** (1998) provide some evidence that the use of economic value measures in compensation plans is associated with the measures' effectiveness. The only subsample in which EVA outperformed traditional accounting measures in predicting stock returns was made of firms using EVA in compensation plans. Similarly, the Sibson & Co. survey (see Table 3.1) indicates that 26.3% of firms using economic value measures in incentive plans reported that these measures were "very successful" and 36.8% reported that they were "marginally successful." None of the respondents stated that the measures were "not successful." The 31.5% of respondents who were "not sure" of the measures' effectiveness were all recent adopters.

**Wallace** (1997) also identified a group of 36 firms that used a residual income measure to some extent in their decision making, but did not include the measure in their incentive compensation. On this sample the same tests performed in the main sample were repeated. The results are generally weaker for these firms (than for the 40 adopters in compensation plans), with only significant results observed for the asset disposition test. The observed results for the financing, operating, and residual income tests are all insignificant. These results support the contention that residual income-based performance measures only work if they are used in compensation plans.

**Wallace's** (1998) survey of EVA users found that firms including EVA in their incentive compensation plans also implemented the measure to a significantly greater degree for capital budgeting and dividend decisions, but not for asset disposal, working capital management, share repurchase, or financing decisions. Firms using EVA in incentive plans also reported significantly greater awareness of the cost of capital, reduced the average accounts receivable age, increased the use of debt, increased sales revenues and had a longer accounts payable cycle. However, changes in the degree of selectivity in the choice of new investment projects, inventory turnover, share repurchases, and debt repayment, were not statistically different in the two EVA user groups.

## References

Balachandran SV (2006) How does residual income affect investment? The role of prior performance measures. Manag Sci 52:383–394

Biddle GC, Bowen RM, Wallace JS (1997) Does EVA beat earnings? Evidence on associations with stock returns and firm values. J Accoun Econ 24:301–336

Biddle GC, Bowen RM, Wallace JS (1998) Economic value added: some empirical evidence. Manag Finance 24:60–71

Chari L (2009) Measuring value enhancement through economic value added: evidence from literature. IUP J Appl Finance 15:46–62

Chen S, Dodd JL (1997) Economic value added (EVA): an empirical examination of a new corporate performance measure. J Manag Issues 9:318–333

Clinton BD, Chen S (1998) Do new performance measures measure up? Manag Accoun 38:40–43

Copeland T (2002) Want to create value? Strateg Finance 83:48–54

Copeland T, Dolgoff A (2006) Expectations-based management. J Appl Corp Finance 18:82–97

Credit Suisse-HOLT (2011) Credit suisse HOLT valuesearch reference handbook. www.credit-suissecom/holtemethodology

Daly K (2011) Corporate performance metrics to top board agendas. Finan Exec 27(1):50–53

Damodaran A (2000) Value creation and enhancement: back to the future. Stern School of Business, New York

Das D, Thomas S, Repetto R (2007) Integrated environmental and financial performance metrics for investment analysis and portfolio management. Corp Gov Inter Rev 15:421–423

Dillon RD, Owers JE (1997) EVA as a financial metric: attributes utilization and relationship to NPV. Finan Pract Educ 7:32–40

Dixon P, Hedley B (1993) Managing for Value. Braxton Associates, Boston

Easton P, Harris T (1991) Earnings as explanatory variable for returns. J Accoun Res 29:19–36

Fernandez P (2002) Three residual income valuation methods and discounted cash flow valuation, SSRN WP 296945

Fernandez P (2003) EVA economic profit and cash value added do NOT measure shareholder value creation. ICFAI J Appl Finance 9:74–94

Forker J, Powell R (2008) A comparison of error rates for EVA residual income GAAP-earnings and other metrics using a long-window valuation approach. Eur Account Rev 17:471–502

Hertz DB (1964) Risk analysis in capital investment. Harvard Bus Rev 42:95–106
Hogan CE, Lewis CM (2005) Long-run investment decisions operating performance and shareholder value creation of firms adopting compensation plan based on economic profits. J Finan Quant Anal 40:721–745
Institute of Management Accountants (IMA) (1996) Are corporate America's financial measurements outdated? Montvale
Ittner CD, Larcker DF (1998) Innovations in performance measurement: trends and research implications. J Manag Accoun Res 10:205–238
Jackson A (1996) The how and why of EVA at CS First Boston. J Appl Corp Finance 9:98–103
Kleiman R (1999) Some new evidence on EVA companies. J Appl Corp Finance 12:80–92
Kramer JK, Peters JR (2001) An inter-industry analysis of economic value added as a proxy for market value added. J Appl Finance 11:41–49
Lehn K, Makhija AK (1997) EVA, accounting profits and CEO turnover: an empirical examination 1985–1994. J Appl Corp Finance 10:90–97
Madden BJ (2007) For better corporate governance the shareholder value review. J Appl Corp Finance 19:102–114
Milunovich S, Tsuei A (1996) EVA in the computer industry. J Appl Corp Finance 9:104–115
Myers R (1996) The metric wars. CFO Mag Chief Finan Off 12:41–50
O'Byrne SF (1996) EVA and market value. J Appl Corp Finance 9:116–125
O'Byrne SF (1997) Eva and shareholder return. Finanl Pract Educ 7:50–54
O'Byrne S, Young SD (2006) Incentives and investor expectations. J Appl Corp Finance 18:98–105
Obrycki DJ, Resendes R (2000) Economic margin: the link between EVA and CFROI. In: Fabozzi FJ, Grant L (eds) Value-Based Metrics: foundations and practice. Wiley, New York
Rappaport A (1986) Creating shareholder value: a guide for managers and investors. Free Press, New York
Rappaport A (1999) New thinking on how to link executive pay with performance. Harvard Bus Rev 2:91–101
Ryan HE, Trahan EA (2007) Corporate financial control mechanisms and firm performance: the case of value-based management systems. J Bus Finance Accoun 34:111–138
Stern JM, Stewart GB, Chew DH (1995) The EVA financial management system. J Appl Corp Finance 8:32–46
Stewart GB (1991) The Quest for Value. Harper Business, New York
Stewart GB (1995) EVA works —But not if you make these common mistakes. Fortune 131:117
Thomas R (1993) Replication of Stern Stewart market value added (MVA) versus economic value added (EVA): empirical results, BCG/HOLT Planning Associates
Wallace JS (1997) Adopting residual income-based compensation plans: Do you get what you pay for? J Accoun Econ 24:275–301
Wallace JS (1998) EVA financial systems: management perspectives. Adv Manag Accoun 6:1–15
Weissenrieder F (1998) Value based management: economic value added or cash value added? Gothenburg studies in financial economics 971214. www.valueanalitix.com—Comparison of methodologies

# Chapter 4
# Concluding Remarks: Strengths and Weaknesses of the Economic Value Measures

**Abstract** In this chapter some concluding remarks are given in order to summarize the main similarities and differences among the economic value measures analyzed in the previous chapters. Their strengths and weaknesses are discussed from the following standpoints: pitfalls in calculation, (in)consistency with value creation, pointing out the potential games which each metric can induce in managerial behaviors, and adequacy for managerial compensation in terms of clearness and verifiability.

**Keywords** Calculation shortcomings of the economic value measures · Old plant trap · Capital game · Risk game · Hurdle rate problem · Short termism

## 4.1 Introduction

If all value-based metrics have similar objectives, why are there different metrics? We might cynically answer that this gives all the consultants something to argue about. However, we could also conclude that different metrics are designed to serve different purposes.

The principal users of value-based metrics are fund managers and equity analysts, on the one hand, and corporate executives, on the other. Each party has unique needs and access to information when conducting its activities. Funds and equity analysts need a metric that allows them to quickly evaluate a large number of companies on the basis of publicly available information (Obrycki and Resendes 2000). They evaluate management's skills by looking at management's historic and forecasted track record relative to peers, and thus determine whether the firm is over or undervalued based on their expectations.

D. Venanzi, *Financial Performance Measures and Value Creation: The State of the Art*, SpringerBriefs in Business, DOI: 10.1007/978-88-470-2451-9_4,

On the contrary, corporate executives have almost limitless information on a single firm. The firm, however, includes many business units, projects and employees. Moreover, corporate executives must not only make strategic decisions to create shareholder value; they must also promote and infuse value-based management principles through the organization down to the lowest levels and they must design and maintain internal management systems to ensure that the firm does not depart from the designated path. Although always aware of the external context (market and competitors), the corporate executive's main focus is internal, with a primary emphasis on managing the operational aspects of running a business. In short, fund managers and analysts want a performance metric that is comparable across a large number of firms and a valuation system that objectively sets target values. Corporate executives want the same properties, but are much more interested in a simple measure that is easy to communicate and administer through the firm.

In the following section we compare the five metrics here analyzed, summarizing their main differences and similarities with reference to some relevant perspectives. A discussion of the leading features follows, with particular regard to the main value-based measures such as EVA, CFROI and SVA. Being EM and CVA combinations of the basic metrics, their strengths and weaknesses, when not directly discussed, can be easily derived comparing their similarities or differences with the main metrics.

## 4.2 A Quick Comparison of the Economic Value Measures

Preliminarily, we can make some general considerations.

Firstly, although with different emphasis, we can observe that all the measures focus the attention on "surplus" value. This concept does stress that it is not how much income a firm makes that proves its success, but how much it makes in excess of its cost of capital. This surplus can be expressed in terms of the well-known NPV approach (such as in the SVA) along the entire expected life of the investment or strategy or, alternatively, in terms of a periodical excess amount (such as in the EVA, EM and CVA) or excess rate (such as in the CFROI) with respect to the capital charge. It is useful to observe that, for this aspect, the residual income-based metrics do not really innovate with respect to the classical NPV approach. In fact, the claim that the residual income measures value creation and the DCF method does not is false because the discounting process "takes into account" value creation.

In addition, it has been noted that making the excess measure an absolute figure (rather than a spread of rates as in CFROI) it helps firms recognize that refusing projects that earn more than their cost of capital (just because they earn less—or a smaller spread—than the existing projects) can destroy value.

Secondly, from the empirical evidence, a univocal and undoubted superior performance of any of the analyzed metrics in predicting shareholder return or market value does not emerge. Theoretically, all the metrics can be reconciled with the DCF approach and therefore can be related to the firm value, more or less directly. However, this reconciliation holds only in *a long-term horizon* and when we consider *all the factors* in which the firm value can be broken down. Therefore, the attempt to define metrics that can be measured on annual basis can appear to be useless if the complete streams of EVA or CFROI or EM over a long period are necessary to evaluate the performance in terms of value creation; or, alternatively, when complex methods to extend the application of these metrics over long horizons are proposed to provide managers with undistorted incentives. Paradoxically, the single-year focus of the EVA and of the other residual income based measures, which seems to be a sound feature, does turn into their major potential drawback.

Thirdly, the corporate use of financial performance measures is a mix of two apparently different perspectives: backward-looking, when we want to measure managerial performance and thus provide the correct incentives to managerial decision-making, and forward-looking, when we want to measure the corporate value based on the present value of future cash flows. The economic value measures analyzed here are intended for both forward- and backward-looking applications. However, they implement that in different ways. EVA and CFROI are skewed towards the backward-looking and catch up the forward-looking perspective by means of the present value of future streams of EVAs and CFROIs in order to reconcile with the DCF approach.

By contrast, SVA gives priority to the forward-looking perspective, consistent with value creation economics, and retrieves the backward-looking in terms of difference between actual and expected SVA (superior SVA), using a sort of hindsight forward-looking approach. The consequences are clear: EVA and CFROI risk to bias managerial incentives by separating the past and current components of the financial performance from the future one; SVA assures the consistency of managerial decisions with the value creation goal but it sets targets and measures past and current managerial performance in a more complex and subjective way.

Now, we will compare the metrics following the different perspectives listed in Table 4.1.

**(a) calculation shortcomings**

As discussed earlier, a primary goal of the value-based metrics is to eliminate the numerous *distortions in the accounting data* in order to provide comparability across time, firms and industries. Once we have cleaned up the accounting data, we can assess if companies are creating or destroying shareholder wealth, and provide more insightful valuations.

EVA, CFROI and EM are partially similar from this perspective. On the contrary, the SVA and CVA directly use in computation the DCF approach, and do not introduce accounting distortions.

However, EVA is the metric that most depends on accounting measures of operating income and capital invested, even though adjustments are made to both,

**Table 4.1** Comparing the economic value measures

| Perspectives of comparison | EVA | CFROI | SVA | EM | CVA |
|---|---|---|---|---|---|
| 1. Shortcomings in calculation | | | | | |
| Accounting distortions | ■ | □ | | □ | |
| Inflation distortion | ■ | | | | |
| IRR traps | | ■ | | | |
| Incomparability across time/industry/firms | ■ | | ■ | | ■ |
| 2. (In)consistency with value creation | | | | | |
| Old plant trap | ■ | | | | |
| Hurdle rate problem | | ■ | | | |
| Capital game | ■ | ■ | | ■ | |
| Short-termism | ■ | ■ | | ■ | |
| Risk incentive | ■ | ■ | | ■ | |
| Explicit linkage with value drivers | | | ■ | | □ |
| Terminal value/perpetuity problem | □ | □ | ■ | □ | □ |
| Applicability in capital rationing | | ■ | | ■ | □ |
| 3. (In)adequacy in managerial compensation | | | | | |
| Clearness and communicability | | | ■ | □ | □ |
| Verifiability | □ | □ | □ | □ | □ |
| Subjectivity | □ | □ | ■ | □ | □ |

□/■ weak/strong presence of the character

as demonstrated by a very strong relationship between adjusted and unadjusted EVA (Anderson et al. 2005). In addition, unlike CFROI and EM, EVA subtracts depreciation in both the earnings portion and investment portion of the calculation. The logic is that the whole annual charge for using capital (in terms of both depreciation and financial charge) should reduce the annual measure of performance

Moreover, unlike CFROI and EM, EVA does not correct the *effect of inflation.*

These features can cause many difficulties for a manager who is trying to compare firms across time and industries, in order to identify the best investment opportunity. For example, how does a manager compare the EVA for two firms when these use different schemes of depreciation? Or when firms have similar fixed assets which were purchased at different times? The major problem is that the profile of the EVAs is dependent on the depreciation schedule: therefore, the interpretation of the profile of the residual income (in terms of both annual levels and year-to-year changes) becomes problematic and leaves room for manipulation (in order to achieve the desired residual income profile). In addition, when we reconcile the EVA approach with the DCF approach, we assume that the depreciation considered in EVA's calculations equals tax depreciation: if this equation does not hold, the reconciliation of the present value of EVAs with the present value of cash flows needs the inclusion of a term for the difference between the tax depreciation and the EVA depreciation, the calculation becoming more complex. Furthermore, the manager must determine if the net asset base adequately accounts for the money the firm has invested to generate its cash flows (e.g. the firm may have fully depreciated, but not retired fixed plant), and whether the depreciation expense is sufficient to replace the existing fixed assets.

CFROI and EM are stated to be focused on cash flows. This is true since non-cash charges are added back to arrive at the gross cash flow and the economic depreciation, and the accounting depreciation is not included; however, the cash flow used in calculations is not the cash flow available for claimholders in the firm, since it is before the capital expenditures and it is stated in real terms.

Unlike EVA, the CFROI is an internal rate of return and not a measure of economic profit. This attribute should favor its *comparability among companies* regardless of their size. This characteristic made the CFROI very popular in the fund managers and analysts' community, as investors need to compare many companies against each other, in order to make investments decisions. As a rate of return, the CFROI is well designed as a tool to assist the institutional investors in picking stocks: for this purpose, they need a systematic means of sorting through the historical data of thousands of businesses to identify potentially undervalued companies and to be able to back test the predictive ability of the model.

By contrast, adopting for this purpose an economic metric like SVA or CVA, for example, would simply be too time consuming, because we would need to separate yearly cash flow estimates, cost of capital and forecast periods for each company.

Also the EM is a rate, and like CFROI is not influenced by size; furthermore, incorporating the investors' required return on capital within its capital charge, it allows a more direct comparison among equities and investments with different risks.

By focusing on the gross investment, rather than the net, and adjusting for current dollars, it is argued that the CFROI provides a superior measure of return on an investment. This argument, however, tends to work better for manufacturing firms but does not really hold up for firms that are not capital intensive. Furthermore, it is argued that by assuming a fixed life for an asset and computing an internal rate of return, the CFROI provides a better measure of return than traditional accounting measures which often divide current earnings by the investment's book value. This, again, is a far better argument with capital intensive firms that invest in plant and equipment, than for firms that invest in short term and intangible assets. Furthermore, if we assume that assets have infinite lives and that capital maintenance expenditures offset depreciation, the CFROI measure converges on the return on capital.

However, as well as IRR, CFROI suffers for the IRR traps in comparing alternatives: given two investments with equal NPV but differing in timing and scale of cash flows, the IRR will often produce different and contradictory answers.

**(b) (in)consistency with value creation**

EVA is distorted by the effect of the *old plant trap* (Obrycki and Resendes 2000) since, like the traditional accounting measures of return, it tends to be overstated because it looks at the remaining book value of assets (net plant). Thus, as assets are depreciated and get older, EVA increases. This doesn't depend on a change of the project's economics: the basic EVA figure increases only because the plant was depreciated, which decreased the capital charge each year. Furthermore, while varying during the investment's expected life, which EVA is the "correct" one, and how does a manager know whether to accept or reject the project? This calculation issue has serious implications on the management incentive mechanism. If a company adopts a compensation system that rewards improvements in EVA, managers are likely to resist growing, since each new project will incrementally decrease their EVA, while doing nothing increases it. Inflation makes the problem even worse, since new investments are expressed at current prices. EVA can deal with the "old plant trap" by replacing the accounting depreciation with the annuity (economic) depreciation, as CFROI and EM do. Obviously, such a solution is not so easy, further for external analysts.

Based on cash flow and gross plant, the EM does not change with time. A project manager rewarded on EM has no conflict regarding growth since new projects are added to the capital base at gross costs, like the other investments, and depreciation is added to net income in order to obtain cash flow.

CFROI suffers the *hurdle rate problem*, when companies set an acceptable rate of return (the cost of capital) and assess performance based on the actual rate achieved. Thus, companies are discouraged from investing in projects that would be expected to achieve a lower return, compared to the currently employed assets, even if the return exceeds the hurdle rate. Investing would result in a greater positive cash flow for the company, but in a lower total rate on the portfolio of investments, lowering the overall performance evaluation criterion. The approval of the project would be discouraged even though the investment would benefit the whole company.

Since the EM is an absolute measure of profit, it should ensure that managers always pursue opportunities that create wealth, eliminating the conflicts created by the IRR based framework.

Both EVA and CFROI (and consequently EM) could be inconsistent with value creation, as demonstrated in Sect. 3.4. Both can provide managers with the incentives to make value destruction decisions in order to meet or to beat the target performance measure. The value of a firm, as showed in Sect. 3.3, can be expressed in terms of value of the assets in place and value of the expected future growth. The value of the assets in place, in turn, depends on the capital invested in them and, respectively, on the EVAs by these assets or the CFROIs on these assets, over their remaining life.

Whenever managers are rewarded on the basis of a single component of the firm value and not of *all* the components, they receive strong incentives to make decisions that decrease value.

The first case is represented by the *capital game*. When managers are judged based on the EVA or CFROI of the assets in place, they will have strong incentives to keep the invested capital down. Since the firm value depends on both the components (EVA or CFROI, on the one hand, and invested capital, on the other), the net effect on value could deceive the expectations.

The second case is represented by the *short-termism*. Whenever managers are judged on the basis of the EVA or CFROI in the current year, or year-to-year changes, or even relative to expectations, they may willingly sacrifice long term competitiveness in the interest of pursuing short-term targets. In other words, managers can be induced to increase the EVA or the CFROI from the assets in place at the expense of future growth: this would happen at expense of the EVAs or CFROIs on future investments, shortening the period of excess return; for example, in the case of CFROI, by affecting the fade factor in terms of speed and abruptness with which CFROI fades toward the cost of capital. However, note that, unlike the ROIC in the EVA, the CFROI is calculated on the basis of a multiple-period idea.

Furthermore, when we consider the cascade throughout the entire organization, being EVA skewed towards the assets in place and away from future growth, it should not be surprising that the higher growth divisions end up with the lowest EVA. Although these divisional managers may still be judged based upon changes in EVA from year to year, the temptation at the firm level to reduce or eliminate capital invested in these divisions will be strong, since it will make the firm's overall EVA increase (Damodaran 2000).

The third case is represented by the *risk game*, when there is a trade-off between the increase of the current EVA or CFROI and the increase of riskiness of future investments and therefore of their cost of capital, that reduces the present value of growth.

Unlike EVA and CFROI, the SVA (and partially the CVA) approach does not suffer these bias. It uses complete information and explicitly incorporates in its analysis historical, current and forecast information in determining the amount and timing of future cash flows, the value growth duration, and systematic and specific risk. Furthermore, it directly measures how changes in strategy will affect the company's value, and its relationship with firm value is clearly indicated to the corporate planners, bringing their attention on the leading long term value drivers.

Conversely, the EVA seems to ignore the firm's core competencies, providing little actionable information on the long-term value drivers.

While it is a useful tool for picking up stocks, the CFROI is less useful for corporate planning. Based on a series of average assumptions in order to avoid explicit forecasts, the CFROI will miss the distinctions. Corporate planners want to understand how changes in strategy will affect their company's value. If a company is characterized by an average strategy, an average investment policy, an average level of systematic risk, and its strategy is not going to change, then the CFROI approach will model this firm effectively. For any company that is not average on all these aspects, the CFROI model will miss the distinctions. For example, would a natural resources company really want to "fade" to the same

CFROI and asset growth as a computer company? The HOLT's model would assume that, although the rates of return and investment growth vary significantly from firm to firm and from industry to industry (www.valueanalitix.com). A value-based system using the CFROI will be unsuccessful without a value driver analysis that unbundles it into discrete and controllable financial and operational variables (Snyder 1995).

However, a weakness of the SVA is its excessive sensitivity to the *residual value*. The residual value can represent the largest part of the created value, for example in a firm with a perpetuity growth greater than zero. It strongly depends on the cash flow in the last forecast period and on the growth in perpetuity assumption: both variables imply subjective and unverifiable estimates, potentially open to manipulation.

As a matter of the fact, also the other metrics suffer the *perpetuity problem*, more or less explicitly. As far as the EVA is concerned, the perpetuity issue regards the length of period of positive EVAs and no guide the EVA approach provides to estimate it. In the CFROI model, the perpetuity problem is solved in terms of the fade factor, and some insights for forecasting it can be derived empirically in different industries by observing the CFROI's historical dynamics, although at the generic industry-level. Similarly, the EM model assumes a decay percentage. In the CVA model the perpetuity assumption is implicit in calculating the operating cash flow demand (OCFD).

There are some firms with significant *capital rationing* constraints, in which it is critical that investments be directed to those projects where they earn the highest possible returns for. For these firms, it can be argued that the value added measures that focus on absolute value may lead to a misallocation of resources, since they implicitly assume that there is sufficient capital to undertake all the good projects. Using a rate of return, such as the CFROI, EM or CVA index, can allow these firms to get the maximum return from a limited capital.

**(c) (in)adequacy in managerial compensation**

Since the SVA's focus is on future performance, it is difficult to apply it when measuring historic performance and then it could be considered less adequate in compensation systems. Compared to EVA, CFROI and EM, the SVA approach is likely to pose less directly the most important question in performance measurement: whether a company earns on its investment a better return than its cost of capital. However, the superior SVA expressed as a difference between actual and expected SVA, in a medium term span, should correctly orient the operating managers to find strategies with the highest potential for increasing value, avoiding the short-term performance obsession. However, building a compensation system based on SVA is clearly not very simple. In addition, the SVA approach can be very subjective, because it incorporates managerial judgement and strategic thinking, and involves specific forecasts about operating factors into the future. The SVA's subjectivity colud seriously undermine the verifiability of the target and reliable measurements in compensation systems, although the other approaches avoid this subjectivity only at the cost of relying on historical data and applying restrictive assumptions about the future.

In any case, when used at the divisions, or strategic business units' level, all metrics, which require the allocation of invested capital or costs to the sub-units, become inevitably subjective and unverifiable, being both the allocation and the required transfer prices contentious and arbitrary. Possible misallocations are likely to reflect the power of individual divisions in influencing the process.

By contrast, a breakdown of the SVA's drivers could be easily used in compensation and in operations evaluation for middle managers and frontline employees, who need to know which specific actions they should take to increase the SVA, being SVA too broad to provide them with much day-to-day guidance. For more specific measures, companies can develop leading indicators of value, which are quantifiable, easily communicated, and directly influenced by frontline managers (Rappaport 1999).

EVA has been criticized for being too complex to be used by frontline managers. For example, AT&T was once touted as a leading proponent of EVA, but has since abandoned this measure (Ittner and Larcker 1998). In 1992, the firm adopted EVA for decision-making and compensation purposes, and implemented an EVA-based bonus plan. Later, EVA was supplemented by two new nonfinancial measures ("customer value added" and "people value added", based on customers' satisfaction and employee's satisfaction, respectively) and was abandoned altogether in 1997 in favor of traditional accounting measures. One primary reason for the measure's demise in AT&T was identified (Ittner and Larcker 1998) in its complexity for most employees to understand, even though AT&T had made relatively few of the accounting adjustments recommended by Stern Stewart. Despite extensive training in the computation and use of the EVA, employees outside of corporate headquarters did not understand how their actions affected EVA results, and felt they had limited ability to impact on EVA's corporate or business unit targets.

This criticism can be partially extended to CFROI, because of the underlying non-linear IRR model of calculation and the difficulty for a manager to link the improvements in cash flow needed to meet the target increase. Also EM and CVA could appear complex to a certain degree, due to the difficulty in calculating the capital charge and the OCFD factor, respectively.

## References

Anderson AM, Bey RP, Weaver SC (2005) Economic value added adjustments: much to do about nothing? WP- Lehigh University

Damodaran A (2000) Value creation and enhancement: back to the future. Stern School of Business, New York

Ittner CD, Larcker DF (1998) Innovations in performance measurement: trends and research implications. J Manag Acc Res 10:205–238

Obrycki DJ, Resendes R (2000) Economic margin: the link between EVA and CFROI. In: Fabozzi FJ, Grant L (eds) Value-based metrics: foundations and practice. Wiley, New York

Rappaport A (1999) New thinking on how to link executive pay with performance. Harvard Bus Rev 2:91–101

Snyder AV (1995) Value-based management: highlighting the resource allocation challenge. Braxton Associates, Boston

www.valueanalitix.com—Comparison of methodologies

# Appendix 1
# Formulas of CFROI

Starting from the following formula

$$GI = GCFa_{n|CFROI} + \frac{SV}{(1 + CFROI)^n}$$

we can demonstrate how the following alternative formulation of the *CFROI* can be derived, if we assume in the calculation of economic depreciation a discount rate $k = CFROI = r$

$$CFROI = (Gross\ Cash\ Flow - Economic\ Depreciation)/Gross\ Investment$$

Stating that:

$$ED = economic\ depreciation = (GL - SV) \times s_{n|r}$$

where $s_{n|r} = [(1 + r)^n - 1]/r$ is the final value of an $n$-period annuity with interest rate $r$

multiplying each member of the above equation by $(1+r)^n$ and therefore subtracting from each member *GI*, we can rewrite the relationship as follows:

$$GI[(1 + r)^n - 1] = GCF \times s_{n|r} - ED \times s_{n|r}.$$

Being $[(1 + r)^n - 1] = r \times s_{n|r}$ and $a_{n|r} = s_{n|r} \times (1 + r)^n$, we can get

$r \times GI = GCF - ED$ therefore $r = (GCF - ED)/GI$ (quod erat demonstrandum)

D. Venanzi, *Financial Performance Measures and Value Creation: The State of the Art*,
SpringerBriefs in Business, DOI: 10.1007/978-88-470-2451-9,

# Appendix 2
# Excess Investor Return in Terms of EVA

According to O'Byrne (1997), we can express the excess investor return in year 1 as follows: $MV_1 + FCF_1 - (1 + k)MV_0$.

Expressing FCF (free cash flow) and MV (market value) in terms of EVA, we can write:

$$MV_0 = cap_0 + EVA_0/k + ((1+k)/k)\sum_{i=1}^{\infty} x_0 \Delta EVA_i/(1+k)^i$$

$$FCF_i = NOPAT_1 - \Delta cap_1 = EVA_i + kcap_0 - \Delta cap_1$$

$$MV_1 = cap_1 + EVA_1/k + ((1+k)/k)\sum_{i=2}^{\infty} x_1 \Delta EVA_i/(1+k)^{i-1}$$

where $x_0 \Delta EVA_i$ and $x_1 \Delta EVA_i$ are the investors's expectations, at the end of year 0 and 1, of EVA improvement in year $i$.

Collecting similar terms and simplifying, we obtain the following relation of the excess return in year 1:

$$((1+k)/k)((EVA_1 - EVA_0) - x_0 \Delta EVA_1) + ((1+k)/k)$$
$$\sum_{i=2}^{\infty} (x_1 \Delta EVA_i - x_0 \Delta EVA_i)/(1+k)^{i-1}$$

Generalizing, we can express the $n$ year excess return as follows:

$$((1+k)/k)((EVA_n - EVA_{n-1}) - x_0 \Delta EVA_n) + ((1+k)/k)$$
$$\sum_{i=n+1}^{\infty} (x_n \Delta EVA_i - x_0 \Delta EVA_i)/(1+k)^{i-n}$$

D. Venanzi, *Financial Performance Measures and Value Creation: The State of the Art*, SpringerBriefs in Business, DOI: 10.1007/978-88-470-2451-9,

Printed by Printforce, the Netherlands